IMPROVING YOUR CLASSROOM TEACHING

SURVIVAL SKILLS FOR SCHOLARS

Managing Editor: Mitchell Allen

Survival Skills for Scholars provides you, the professor or advanced graduate student working in a college or university setting, with practical suggestions for making the most of your academic career. These brief, readable guides will help you with skills that you are required to master as a college professor but may have never been taught in graduate school. Using hands-on, jargon-free advice and examples, forms, lists, and suggestions for additional resources, experts on different aspects of academic life give invaluable tips on managing the day-to-day tasks of academia—effectively and efficiently.

Volumes in This Series

SURVIVAL SKILLS FOR SCHOLARS

IMPROVING YOUR CLASSROOM TEACHING

M A R Y E L L E N   W E I M E R

SAGE Publications
International Educational and Professional Publisher
Newbury Park   London   New Delhi

Copyright © 1993 by Sage Publications, Inc.

For information address:

 SAGE Publications, Inc.
2455 Teller Road
Newbury Park, California 91320

SAGE Publications Ltd.
6 Bonhill Street
London EC2A 4PU
United Kingdom

SAGE Publications India Pvt. Ltd.
M-32 Market
Greater Kailash I
New Delhi 110 048 India

Printed in the United States of America

Library of Congress Cataloging-in-Publication Data

Main entry under title:

Weimer, Maryellen, 1947-
 Improving your classroom teaching / Maryellen Weimer
      p.   cm.   — (Survival skills for scholars ; vol. 1)
 Includes bibliographical references.
 ISBN 0-8039-4975-8 — ISBN 0-8039-4976-6 (pbk.)
 1. College teaching—United States. I. Title. II. Series.
LB2331.W38   1993
378.1'25—dc20   93-24839

  94   95   96   10   9   8   7   6   5   4   3   2

Sage Production Editor: Megan M. McCue

For Gabriele Bauer, a colleague, friend,
and exceptional mentor of new college teachers

Contents

Introduction

It is difficult and to some degree preposterous to try in 130 pages to tell new teachers what they need to know about a phenomenon as complicated as teaching. But for new college teachers it is realistic to try. Academic positions require new faculty to execute in a hurry a whole set of instructional tasks: course planning, textbook selection, test construction, advising, lecturing, and using group work, among others. These are not tasks for which most faculty are trained, and they must be executed in a hurry. The first day of class will not be canceled because some new faculty member has yet to complete a course syllabus.

So for the new academic, "survival" ends up being a key concept, a modus operandi. If the rest of my teaching career was as frenetic, stressful, and downright dissatisfying as my first year, I most certainly would not be writing this text. But I made it; so will you, and subsequent years will be better.

However, I would have been helped during those first teaching years by knowledge acquired subsequently. It is true that you learn some of the most important lessons about teaching by experience. But in the academic profession we rely too much on experiential learning. Virtually everything we learn about teaching we learn while doing it. As a result, most of our understandings are intuitive, not easily articulated, and therefore not shared with new teachers who must struggle to once again reinvent the wheel.

This book aims to intervene. It provides faculty with fundamental, bottom-line information about teaching and learning. There are things you should and shouldn't do, there is research relevant to a number of key instructional decisions, there are mistakes to be avoided, and best of all, there are other resources and information that you can turn to.

As practical and concrete as is its approach, the book still leaves a myriad of questions unanswered. These questions open our eyes to the complex, intriguing, and intellectually robust aspects of the teaching-learning phenomenon. The educational enterprise continues to be devalued by our society, our academic institutions, and even by us. I think part of the problem is caused by the simplistic way we think about it. The phenomenon of effective instruction involves much more than a bag of tricks.

The book's chapters are organized around research-identified components, or ingredients of effective instruction. I decided on that structure because those components create a context that makes the teaching tasks a part of something larger and focuses on techniques as means rather than instructional ends. The research-identified components of instruction constitute an operational definition of good teaching, and we know that good teaching has powerful (and measurable) effects on student learning. So we will frame our discussion of teaching around the components of effective instruction and let teaching tasks and techniques serve this larger context.

Individual chapters focus on each of the five research-identified components of effective instruction: enthusiasm, preparation and organization, the ability to stimulate thought and interest, clarity, and knowledge and love of the content. Along with the concrete strategies and identification of underlying issues, the chapters compare the components and propose ways they relate to and reinforce one another. Because good teaching results in student learning, the book concludes by turning the tables and proposes that our efforts to assess student learning produce measures of our instructional effectiveness.

This book is but another sequel in my career-long love affair with teaching. It all started in the fourth grade when I taught a third grader to read. Never mind that I threatened him with all manner of punishments or that I diagnosed the problem as laziness. I did figure out that his teachers had yet to give him a book he wanted to read. I found one and refused to tell him how it ended. I took great pride in his success and looked at what my teachers did with a new sense of interest.

In college a wonderful advisor, who listened to my complaints about education classes and who let me team teach in several class periods with him, said to me one day, "You know, you could be a professor." I learned to teach at Linfield College, a small private institution in Oregon. I had several mentors and a host of wonderful colleagues who, when they asked, "How are your courses going?" were interested in the truth and were willing to talk the "stuff" of teaching: strategies, techniques, ideas, issues, information, questions, and answers.

My early teaching experiences raised questions that neither I nor my colleagues answered very well, and gradually my interest in the research and scholarship of teaching took root. I discovered how much we do know about teaching and learning and how that information could improve practice. Next thing I knew I was running a unit with the mandate to support and encourage faculty efforts to maintain and improve instructional quality. Those experiences spawned a spate of publications and presentations and a still unabated interest in the intricacies of the teaching-learning process.

Recently I had the opportunity as part of a research project to interview some first-year college teachers. Their stories reminded me of my own initial efforts. I couldn't believe how much I have learned since then and how much I wanted to share my knowledge with them. This book is for them.

Special thanks to Mitch Allen for his patience and excellent editorial direction; Sheila Petrosky for outstanding clerical support; Ralph E. Lundgren for his assistance in the developmental stages of the book; Gabriele Bauer, whose extensive comments improved the manuscript; and Kelly Parsley, who knows how to keep me sane.

MARYELLEN WEIMER
August 1993

1 | Developing Effective Teaching Skills

Because so many of us start teaching without training or preparation, and because we learn to teach by doing, it's easy to jump to wrong conclusions about effective instruction. Many faculty do this. As they compare how they teach with how their colleagues teach and as they hear about recognized good teachers, they correctly observe that effective instruction comes in lots of different forms. Two erroneous conclusions are often drawn from that observation and that's when problems result. We need to begin our understanding of how effective teaching skills develop by debunking these two myths.

Myth #1: Nobody Knows What Makes Teaching Effective

Some faculty attribute the differences in effective instruction to the eclectic, idiosyncratic nature of the teaching phenomenon—it's like art, variable and unpredictable. Others see the differences as a function of the personality of the teacher; others as some inexplicable combination of the two. Many mistakenly conclude that nobody knows what makes teaching effective. Good teaching is mystery, magic; it happens for an instructor, a course, or class period on the whim

5

of the gods or the alignment of the planets. In other words, the phenomenon controls us as opposed to us having a measure of mastery over it.

Most faculty do not spend a lot of time informing their beliefs and assumptions about teaching. I find this odd, since we hold ourselves so rigorously to the principles of documentation and substantiation in our research. However, as a profession those standards of proof are not applied to what we believe about teaching and learning. Most faculty are unaware that, beginning in the 1930s, researchers have attempted to identify and describe the components of effective instruction.

These researchers, like others who study teaching and learning at the college level, include educational psychologists, sociologists, psychologists, and faculty developers. In their studies of effective instruction, they have collected and analyzed data from students who were at different points in their academic careers and in a wide range of disciplines. They have solicited and studied the opinions of faculty and administrators, as well as trustees and others with knowledge and interest in the subject. The problem, as with any type of research, is that the conclusions vary. Not all the studies found the same components, not all were done with equally valid designs, and nomenclature is used inconsistently.

However, reviews of research, in this case both quantitative and qualitative ones, help us sort through conflicting conclusions and enable us to see where the bulk of the research evidence lies. I've chosen to organize the book around a list of effective instructional components generated by a qualitative review* conducted by Thomas Sherman and a group of colleagues (1986). The Sherman team studied the research in this area and found consistent evidence of five (overlapping and interrelated) components of effective instruction.

---

*AUTHOR'S NOTE: The quantitative reviews use metaanalytic techniques that allow the statistical comparison of results. The best work in the area has been done by Kenneth Feldman (1975, 1988), who identifies 12 components.

Components of Effective Instruction

1. Enthusiasm
2. Preparation and organization
3. Ability to stimulate student thought and interest
4. Clarity
5. Knowledge and love of the content

This book is devoted to an exploration of these five components. Relevant now is the fact that these research findings debunk the myth that nobody knows what makes teaching effective. We not only know, but have lots of evidence to prove it.

Myth #2: Good Teachers Are Born, Not Made

Those who believe this myth see teaching ability as some sort of gift. Some of us have it, but most of us do not. The two myths are related. If you see the wide variations in teaching style, attribute it to the eclectic nature of the phenomenon, and conclude that nobody knows what makes for effective instruction, it is easy to think of teaching excellence as a gift. But a careful look at what appears on the list reveals acquirable skills, not divine gifts. However, the list leaves us with a large unanswered question.

If the components of effective instruction are pretty much consistent across disciplines, teachers, and students, how do we account for the enormous disparity in teaching styles? Quite simply, I think. The attributes of instruction we have mentioned are abstractions; they have no tangible physical properties. You cannot go out and get some enthusiasm. But do we know enthusiasm when we see it? Can we tell an enthusiastic instructor from one who is not? You bet. What causes us to conclude that an attribute is present or not is the presence or absence of certain behaviors we have come to associate with it. Enthusiastic instructors (we could substitute "organized" or any of the other characteristics) do certain things unenthusiastic instructors don't do. I would argue that all effective instructors are enthusiastic but convey that enthusiasm in widely different ways. Some prance around the room, others gesture with energy, some speak loudly, others use penetrating eye contact. The same could be said for clarity: Some use questions to ensure understanding, others tell stories, some use analogies to bridge the familiar and unfamiliar, others pile one example onto another as they build understanding. And we could continue with the other characteristics in exactly the same vein.

Effective Instruction: The Mental Mindset

- It's what you *do*.
- It's a style that fits you.
- It builds on your strengths.

Lurking inside this orientation to teaching are three empowering notions. First, when we describe effective instruction at this very concrete level, we focus on things teachers *do*, and most of them are easily implementable. Extensive graduate preparation is not required to prance around the room, gesture, raise the volume, or use more direct eye contact—just some practice. So, developing an effective teaching style is by no means an impossible proposition.

Second, there is no prescribed set or combination of things you must do in order to convey enthusiasm or any of the other components. The options are limitless. What seems to work best are actions that fit comfortably with who you are and how you communicate generally. What do you do outside the classroom to convey enthusiasm? That repertoire ought to be the foundation of what you decide to do in class.

If you are prone to gesture, gesture in class. If you talk fast, talk faster in class.

So you begin to build your style by doing what comes naturally. If some of the components of effective instruction are not your bailiwick, that does not necessarily relegate you to the ranks of the ineffective, which brings us to the third empowering notion. You need not be equally excellent in all five of the characteristics. The strength of some components seems to compensate for the absence of others. For example, the best teacher I had in my graduate education was undoubtedly the most disorganized prof I have ever encountered. It was the only the class I've ever taken whose syllabus actually said, "Turn in two copies of all assignments. The instructor has a bad habit of losing student work." I found the lack of organization frustrating, but I forgave him. The man taught me how to write. He demystified the writing process and put it firmly under my control. The enthusiasm and vigor with which he tackled our work inspired both our best efforts and a morbid fear that our best might not be good enough. In the end, it did not matter that he was disorganized.

How the components of instruction relate and overlap is not yet well understood, so this notion of compensation should not be taken to mean substitution. The vast majority of teachers cannot get away without some degree of organization and structure to their teaching. Moreover, the absence of the knowledge component raises a serious ethical issue. You might be an effective teacher if you are enthusiastic, prepared, organized, and able to explain clearly and motivate your students, but should you even try if you have no knowledge of the content? Although your teaching style should not lack any of the components, it can be successful even if the components are not equally represented.

To summarize, this mindset allows us to see the common components of effective instruction but explain the differences. The approach empowers new teachers for three reasons. First, when you think about effective instruction concretely, the focus is on things teachers do, most of which are quite easily implemented. Second, because there is no single prescribed set of actions that convey any component of effective instruction, you may (in fact should) choose to do what fits naturally and comfortably with who you are and how you communicate. Finally, you need not worry if some of the aspects of effective instruction come less easily to you. Most good teachers are not equally effective across all five components. They develop a style that plays to their strengths and compensates for their weaknesses.

The Components: Parts—but an Integrated Whole

Even though the context and details of effective teaching are of course more complex than I have represented them, the fact remains that we know the components of effective instruction and they are acquirable skills. It is the central theme of this book and an empowering concept to encounter as one confronts and contemplates college teaching for the first time.

But the first chapter cannot end here. There's a layer to be added to this central fact even before we begin our exploration of each component in terms of its concrete strategies and techniques. Effective instruction is more than just five components operating in isolation. Each one is affected and influenced by the others. They relate to one another and ultimately must join to form an integrated whole.

For example, there is the relative importance of the respective components. Some are more important than others but which ones depends on who you ask. For students, the central ingredient is enthusiasm. It is the one they mention first, the one they say matters most, and the one they think we most need to improve. Faculty, on the other hand, defer to knowledge of the content. What is teaching without "stuff" to teach? It is a sham, a hypocrisy of the highest order.

Other than this beginning bit of detail as to the relative importance of the ingredients, research holds few other answers. We have not studied how the ingredients relate to and overlap with one another. This means we are not in a position to say that, generally, more enthusiasm compensates for less organization or that the ability to stimulate interest is more important than clarity. We do not know if some of these components take precedence over others early in a career, then relinquish that importance as teaching experience accumulates. We do know that new faculty tell us they worry most about their ability to handle the content.

It may in fact be that no overarching topology of relationship exists—that how the components interact and affect one another varies with each individual. Certainly, in terms of the new faculty person trying to get a handle on how to teach, understanding the arrangement of the components on an individual level is a much more interesting and useful notion than contemplating the possibility of some transcendent set of relationships.

To that end, I suggest as you read through this book and think of your own teaching that you try visually representing the relationships between the components. Use a set of circles. Make their size proportional to their importance. Overlap the circles to show areas of interface, such as between love of content and enthusiasm or clarity and knowledge of the content. Use arrows to indicate reciprocal relationships. Does your enthusiasm stimulate student interest?

Let me illustrate this with a diagram of my own teaching (Figure 1). Knowledge of the content, enthusiasm, and the ability to stimulate students are three equal-sized circles, larger than the other two. They are my strengths and all strongly related. I love my content—it is so important and intrinsically interesting that I can't imagine being anything less than widely enthusiastic about it. My enthusiasm and knowledge contribute to my ability to stimulate students. I use anecdotes and illustrations that derive from my knowledge and experience in the field. I also love to tell stories. I put clarity and organization on the other side. They are smaller with organization being the smallest circle. Clarity derives from an intimate

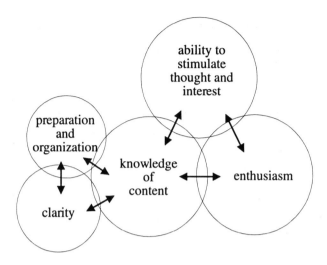

Figure 1.1.

knowledge of the field. I have some of that, but it also derives from organization—understanding how the bits and pieces of knowledge are ordered—and I have less of that. I am not clear because I am not terribly structured. I teach spontaneously, responding with energy to what is happening at the moment. I bounce from one event in class to the next not caring as much as I should that they lead to some conclusion. Cynically summarized, students have a good time in my classes, but too often they are hard pressed to see how it all relates.

Depending on how visually oriented you are, you can spend a lot or a little time constructing your own representation. The idea is to use an activity like this to encourage exploration of the relationships among these components so that you will begin to see how the nuts and bolts of your instructional style fit together. What impresses those of us who regularly observe college teachers is how the effective ones have managed to mold the separate dimensions. They become an integrated whole with integrity and power. That may be too lofty and abstract to be of much practical value, but you need to think about teaching style in terms of fit—how the parts make a whole that genuinely and authentically represents who you are.

The Equation of Fit

In trying to make more concrete the transition from separateness to wholeness, it may help to think of an equation. We have the answer: effective instruction. On the other side of the equation we have the components, but what is unknown is how those component terms function in relation to each other.

And the equation is still more complicated. Effective instruction "fits" the *individual*—it is a suitable, comfortable set of activities, policies, and practices for the teacher involved, but that is not the only relevant "fit." Effective instruction *fits the configuration of the content, the learning needs of students, and the instructional setting.*

Effective Instruction Fits:

- the individual
- the configuration of the content
- the learning needs of students
- the instructional setting

There is no doubt that what we teach has profound impacts on how we teach. You do not discuss themes in a novel the same way you discuss the periodic table. You do not have "right answers" in a literature course the same way you have them in a math course. Although content configuration accounts for some of the variations in teaching style, it does not mean that the ingredients of effective instruction are discipline-specific. In fact, research (Feldman, 1975, 1988) substantiates a consistent, cross-disciplinary set of components. Nonetheless, the methods and actions of instruction reflect the nature and structure of knowledge within a discipline.

Next, instructional style needs to fit the learning needs of the students. The repertoire of strategies, policies, and practices you use must facilitate student learning. You cannot teach like the authoritarian and intimidating Kingfield Fisher of the television series *The Paper Chase* if what you teach is an entry-level, required biology course at an institution with an open admissions policy. You need something more like the enthusiasm and flair for the dramatic of a John Keating in the *Dead Poets Society*.

Often new faculty, fresh from the heady environs of graduate school, have trouble connecting with the learning needs of students. What do they know? How much can they read? How fast can they do problems or complete exams? An effective teacher observes students carefully, solicits feedback from them, and then tailors or fits the instructional policies and practices to their learning needs.

Moreover, the learning needs of students change across their college experience—or at least they should. Assignments in courses for freshmen should not be the same as assignments in courses for seniors. The amount of student autonomy and responsibility for their own learning ought to increase as they gain experience in the college setting.

Finally, the instruction must fit the setting. Is it a large class or small? How long is the period? Is it a lab, lecture, or seminar? Does the room accommodate in-class group work? Variations like these have instructional implications, and the good teacher works to fit course activities to the setting.

Effective instruction, then, is more than your particular brand of being enthusiastic, prepared and organized, clear, stimulating, and knowledgeable. How you teach must fit the configuration of the content, the learning needs of students, and the instructional setting. It is a complicated equation you will spend your career working to solve.

Let me illustrate how this notion of fit might work with the components of organization. Let us be specific: Say the lecture is on causes of the Civil War. You begin by making some decisions based on how you teach. What level of detail do you need in your lecture notes? Are you most comfortable going into class with the three main points in your head and making it happen from there? Or, do you like to present from detailed notes?

Next you need to think about the structure of the content itself. Is it tightly configured, meaning ideas and information build on each other in a linear fashion where any omitted step puts the whole structure in peril? Or is the structure of the material more cosmic, visible only from a distance, spanning lots of isolated details? The second is probably more the case with a lecture on causes of the Civil War. There may be separate reasons, but they became part of a web of influences. Their interdependence would need to be part of the discussion.

At this point, you must integrate into this equation the learning needs of the students. How much structure do they need? If they are beginning students, as they probably would be with this lecture topic, they may not be terribly confident learners, which generally means the more structure the better. Freshmen will probably want to know the "best" or "most important" reason why the Civil War started. Students grow in their ability to tolerate ambiguity. Seniors can be expected to be less linear and more global in their thinking. And learning needs like these vary, not only across the time dimension but also by gender and ethnic background.

Finally, how you teach needs to fit the setting in which you teach. You can get by with much less structure in a senior seminar with 10 students than in an entry-level course with 125. With the big American history class, you might want to list the reasons on an overhead, the board, or on a skeleton lecture outline distributed to students.

Some interesting tensions can develop. What if the content is not tightly structured, like literature survey courses or music appreciation, but the class is large? Or, what if the teacher is best in a spontaneous, free-flowing conversation, but the students are first-year and not at a highly selective institution? In other words, institutional structures such as decisions on class size and who gets to teach what sometimes intervene to make the fit more difficult. Modifications and compromises become necessary, complicating the decisions and making the solution to equation of fit feel illusory.

Conclusion

We have not yet started to explore the components of effective instruction, and we are already well beyond the simple fact with which we began. We identified the components of effective instruction and proposed that they were acquirable skills. We have moved on to show that being a good teacher entails more than a decision to be enthusiastic, organized, clear, stimulating, and knowledgeable. It involves translating those abstract ingredients into tangible behaviors, policies, and practices and then assembling from that wide repertoire of possibilities a set of instructional nuts and bolts that fit the requirements of our own style proclivities, the configuration of our content, the learning needs of our students, and the instructional context in which they will occur. Deciding more about the exact nature of that fit will be easier once we have unpackaged each of the components more fully. But even this early on, our discussion should confirm what you probably already suspect: Learning to teach well requires commitment and hard work.

Background Reading

Author's note: At the conclusion of each chapter, I will list some sources that relate to the topics of the chapter. These are places to turn next if you are ready to learn more about the chapter's content. They should not be confused with specific references cited within the chapter that appear in the reference section at the end of the book.

Browne, M. N., & Keeley, S. M. (1985). Achieving excellence: Advice to new teachers. *College Teaching, 33*(2), 78-83.

Eble, K. A. (1988). *The craft of teaching* (2nd ed.). San Francisco: Jossey-Bass.

Eison, J. (1990). Confidence in the classroom: Ten maxims for new teachers. *College Teaching, 38*(1), 21-24.

Lowman, J. (1984). *Mastering the techniques of teaching.* San Francisco: Jossey-Bass.

McKeachie, W. J. (1986). *Teaching tips* (8th ed.). Lexington, MA: Heath.

Weimer, M. (1990). *Improving college teaching.* San Francisco: Jossey-Bass.

2 | Enthusiasm: The Zest for Teaching

Like several of the other components of effective instruction, enthusiasm is at the same time both simple and complex. At its core, enthusiasm consists of concrete behaviors and specific strategies. It is nuts-and-bolts stuff—essential equipment for the teacher's tool chest. But enthusiasm is much more—a montage of less tangible and more vexing issues. It involves risk, vulnerability, and a willingness to empower students. In addition, enthusiasm seems to sustain teaching in ways that make it less susceptible to burnout. Thinking about enthusiasm in terms of risk, vulnerability, empowerment, and burnout makes the notion of "doing" as a prescribed, daily potion a clearly inadequate solution.

In this chapter we will move between the concrete actions that convey enthusiasm and their inherent complexities. Topics include descriptions of how to communicate enthusiasm, explorations of how enthusiasm involves risk and makes us vulnerable, a list of concrete ways to keep our anxiety under control, and a discussion of the interplay of variables that make it hard to cultivate and sustain the zest for teaching.

Enthusiasm: Do It!

Sometimes faculty have trouble with the word *enthusiasm*. They tell themselves to be enthusiastic and then imagine doing all sorts of things that feel artificial, inauthentic, and awkward. This is style at its affected worst. Not only is the thought repulsive, but the results are equally offensive. Non-verbal behaviors do not lie. They tell our true feelings, which means you cannot fake enthusiasm for long—certainly not for the length of a course. Your students will find you out and think less of you for trying.

The first point: *Do not try to be enthusiastic.* This sounds like ill-conceived advice in light of the established fact that enthusiasm is one of the research-identified components of effective instruction. The verb holds the key: Do not try *to be* enthusiastic. Rather, focus on things you can do that will convey your enthusiasm to the class.

You can (and should) begin by talking about what energizes you as you anticipate the course ahead. Are you pleased to be teaching this course? Why? What is it about this content that intrigues you? What brings you to this institution? To a teaching career in higher education? Most of us are here because we have chosen to be. Letting students know whence we came and why can set the stage for actions that convey enthusiasm.

But a one-liner in the syllabus and/or on the first day falls far short of what is needed to demonstrate enthusiasm. The old adage about actions speaking louder than words could not be truer when it comes to conveying enthusiasm. You must show with actions that you care about the educational enterprise.

At this point the research is helpful. Harry Murray (1983, 1985, 1987), a psychologist at the Western Ontario University, hypothesized what specific behaviors might convey enthusiasm (he's done this for some of the other ingredients of effective instruction as well). With a list of them in hand, he and his research team observed instructors with high and low ratings on enthusiasm on student evaluation forms and discovered he was right. "Enthusiastic" instructors in his sample did some things the "unenthusiastic" instructors did not.

For example, enthusiastic instructors in this research spoke in a dramatic or expressive way. They moved about while lecturing. They gestured with hands or arms and used facial expressions. They walked up the aisles beside students and gestured with their heads or bodies. They told jokes or humorous anecdotes and smiled or laughed while teaching. They did not read from prepared notes or texts and showed no distracting mannerisms.

Sometimes this research leaves people a bit cold because the findings are so obvious, but they do raise an interesting set of follow-up questions. Is this a complete list? Do other behaviors work? What about combinations? How much of any enthusiasm action do you need in order to get the message across that you care? All are appropriate questions and all are unanswered by this and other research. But before we undermine the findings, we need to reaffirm their importance—not so much for the list but for the orientation they prescribe we take toward developing our teaching skills. They tell us that in order to convey enthusiasm, we should not attempt to change what we *are* (which is the distasteful orientation with which we began) but to work on changing what we *do*. Enthusiasm is an attitude made manifest by concrete actions. If you move around the room, gesture, raise your voice, and really look at the students, you will communicate the kind of zest and energy that are part of effective instruction. Said simply: Enthusiasm is something you do!

Braving the Risk

But as empowering and appropriate as the approach is, too much enthusiasm reduces teaching to mechanistic absurdity. Enthusiasm is more complicated than a prescribed set of things you do. Your actions reveal something about you—they show what you think is important. And disclosures of this kind make you vulnerable, especially when you may be the only one present who thinks something is important.

You have spent years of your life studying a specialized area of content. In many respects, it is your life: It gives you value and purpose. Unfortunately most of our specialties are not well understood outside the academy or by our students. It is not obvious what attracts us to these areas of study. So you waltz into the class the first day and tell those present that you study mosses, in fact specialize in mosses of boreal forest, and they may laugh.

I observed a class once in an entry-level English course where students were discussing *Oedipus Rex*. The discussion was labored, with lots of instructor questions, long pauses, followed by short, tentative, student answers. It was clear they thought the story was strange and remained unconvinced that this bizarre tale merited the distinction "classic." At one point the instructor directed the students to a particular passage, which he read aloud with eloquence and feeling. When he finished he looked out at the class and said, "You know, when I read that last night it made me quiver." A stony silence followed. Students looked at each other. He had to be weird. Quiver—that made the man quiver? Nobody else in class had quivered when they read that passage.

They did not laugh. But they also did not understand. They identified with each other and not with him or with Oedipus. He was the odd person out—the one with the unusual response —and as such he was vulnerable. But his admission conveyed an important message. It gave the passage impact. It was interesting to observe the class. After looking at each other with semiconcealed, appalled glances, most of them looked back at the passage. They were rereading it—really reading it for the first time. I suspect they were trying to see what their instructor saw in those words. It was not the same passage anymore. I didn't see any of them quiver, but their instructor's "enthusiasm" had had its effect.

Math courses have never been among my favorites nor has my performance in them been anything to write home about. It's much more a case of having survived an ordeal. As an observer of a math course several years ago, I felt thankful it was not a course I was teaching or taking. The instructor labored with the class through a long proof. The board was full by the time the answer finally emerged. At that point the instructor stepped back from the board and looked at the proof. It was quiet in the room when the instructor commented to no one in particular, "Look at that symmetry. God, that's beautiful, such pure logic." I stared at the board. Symmetry? Beauty? Logic? Where were they? I sure didn't see them. What did the instructor see there that I was missing? He didn't point it out (maybe he should have), but it was an upper-division course and I noticed a number of nods and smiles when he made the observation. Again, it was a simple, unpresupposing kind of comment, but it stopped me short. It had never occurred to me that some folks might see beauty in a math proof.

These examples illustrate something about enthusiasm that goes beyond the concrete list of physical actions with which we started. The advice here is much less specific. If what you've concluded is that you should "quiver" in class and point out the symmetry of your discipline, you've missed the point.

In both examples we are not talking about a particularly dramatic or ostentatious display of emotion. Both were quiet comments, more or less offered in passing. These are not affectations—put on as one dons make-up and a costume before a play so as to disguise the real person. In both cases they came across as honest statements of feelings—genuine, authentic representations of what had been experienced. The problem is not in the skill required to execute but in the willingness to take the risk.

Showing an enthusiastic response to the boreal forests, *Oedipus Rex*, or the symmetry of a mathematical proof takes some courage. You may appear foolish to your students. Good teachers run that risk. Fear constrains most others. They are afraid of students and the power that comes to a class when an instructor exposes a true feeling. It is true that some classes use their power to hurt, but more often something quite the opposite occurs. Your vulnerability touches theirs and they respond. They decide to take a second look—to follow your lead and take risks of their own.

Enthusiasm is the component students regularly identify as the most important ingredient of effective instruction. It has such priority for them because it stimulates, motivates, and involves them. The instructor becomes the plug that connects students with the power source. Our enthusiasm energizes them. They come to care because we have shown them how much we care.

It's Not Nice Being Nervous

I wonder how I would have responded to the preceding examples and discussion when I was a new teacher. I suspect I would consider it a bit beside the point. I was very nervous about teaching.

We are back to the mundane—the pragmatic, practical advice new teachers need to make it through those first few classes. These are all new tasks and you have never done them before, and that makes you nervous, but the underlying anxiety stems from the more deep-seated vulnerabilities and risks we have just described. The first step in coping with anxiety is to recognize the reasons for fear are real. Teaching, like all other jobs, has its share of occupational hazards.

You might be comforted to know that all teachers—even those of us with lots of years in the classroom—experience nervousness to varying degrees. If misery loves company, you've got plenty. For all of us, the goal is the same: to manage and control the anxiety so it does not control and manage us.

Consider these concrete suggestions as methods for gaining control of tension that has the power to tear us apart. First, *become aware of how your nervousness reveals itself.* You can do nothing to control it if you are unaware of its physical manifestations. What's happening to you? Dry mouth? Shaky hands? knees? voice? Are you pacing? Using a repetitive gesture or phrase?

Armed with knowledge of how your nervousness shows, you can respond in one of three ways: *stop it, transfer it,* or *tackle it.* Let's say you hold on to the podium with something akin to a death grip. Whenever you find yourself in that position, force yourself to let go. Relax your hands, spread your fingers, put them in your pockets. Step back, to the side, away from the podium. Keep after yourself. This is a habit you can break. Stop doing it.

If your hands are shaky, try gestures. Relax your arms. Let go of your notes; the tighter you hold them, the more they will shake. Move your hands, use them to emphasize a statement or point out a fact—thereby transferring energy to a more productive and meaningful movement.

Dry mouth? Bring a cup of coffee or have some water up front. Red, overheated face? Unbutton a top button, take off your jacket, or open a window. Afraid to look at students? See if you can locate one or two friendly faces. Begin by speaking to them. Add more students as you warm up. Return to the friendly ones if you feel threatened. In other words, tackle signs of nervousness up front, sensibly.

Now, get on with the show. Do not be debilitated by the fact that you feel nervous—get going, start teaching. Think about the content and the impact you could have on these students. There is truth in another adage about enthusiasm being contagious. As your zest and interest stimulate students, they listen and respond, and their reaction empowers you. Soon you have forgotten to be nervous.

I once observed an entomology class where the instructor was presenting material on water beetles. In fact, this particular lecture was about the back legs of water beetles. I remember sitting in that class and thanking my lucky stars that I did not have to spend my career teaching students about water beetles. I taught things that made a difference, that affected world order. Then I looked around the room and discovered to my amazement that the students appeared interested in water beetles. They were taking notes, nodding in agreement, asking questions, and listening. In fact, they looked much more attentive than students in the class I'd just finished teaching. Then I looked at the teacher. He was totally captivated by his content. He demonstrated how the beetle's back leg hit the water with a bold arm gesture. He raced over to the overhead to fill in part of the drawing he'd missed. He eagerly answered questions. Apparently nobody had told him that millions of Americans cared little, if not at all, about water beetles. He'd studied them for years and found them fascinating. It was an important lesson for me. If he could get students *that* involved with water beetles, I could get them to respond to the paradigms of persuasion.

So the final answer to nervousness is to let go. This feels like the riskiest of all the options when you are nervous. We want to control because we feel a loss of control. But the exact opposite is true. Less control ends up being more control—if you're willing to start by giving it up.

Cultivating and Maintaining Enthusiasm

There are some psychologically draining aspects of teaching that we often reckon with only superficially. Teaching—particularly good teaching—requires a lot of an individual. It's hard, relentless work. Even though you maintain appropriate professional distance from your students, you still get involved with them, care about them, worry when they fail and falter. You find yourself "being there for them" in large and small ways. And then they leave, most of them out of your life forever.

Add to this drain the variety of policies and practices our institutions employ that wear us down. At many of our colleges and universities teaching loads are heavy, and at very few places are class sizes anything but on the rise. Almost universally, students are not as well prepared or motivated as they once were. They are more difficult to teach. Also, at most institutions there are expectations—sometimes high—for scholarly productivity, which almost always directly competes with time spent on teaching.

Add to these pressures the steady and relentless academic calendar. Course follows course, semester after semester. How many sections of that entry-level sociology course will you teach? George Brown (1978) asserts in the beginning of his book *On Lecturing and Explaining* that the "average" (he doesn't specify what that means or how he came to this conclusion) faculty member will deliver 8,000 lectures. That is a lot of lectures, especially when you consider how many courses you teach over and over again.

It may seem inappropriate to be writing about the psychologically draining aspects of teaching at the one point in your career when you probably do not feel burned out and are in fact enthused. However, there are ways of thinking about and approaching teaching tasks that, if set in place at the beginning of the career, will help you overcome the innervating aspects of this profession.

You need to think of teaching as an adventure. It is not something to get figured out once and for all and then teach happily ever after. In fact, even though much about teaching remains the same (the courses you teach, the number you teach, perhaps the time they are offered, their length, and so on), *no class is ever the same*. Even two sections of the same class with the same text, offered back to back, in which you use the same methods and strategies to get through the same content, can be like two different worlds. That makes teaching something of an adventure. Though you make careful plans, following roads you know well, it is still a new trip every time.

The sense of adventure derives not only from the unpredictable surprises but also from the freedom we have to try different roads. The destination always remains the same— student learning—but the ways and means of getting there are limitless. It is easy for teachers to fall into comfortable ruts, and not much in the way of penalty comes to them for that choice. Perhaps in your eager enthusiasm you cannot imagine yourself in a rut? I was astonished and chagrined to discover one year that my opening lecture notes were 13 years old. How had that happened? Well, I liked the opening. I had worked hard on it and students responded well. With the press of everything else at the beginning of the semester I just never seemed to have time to put something else together. But 13 years doing the same thing is too long. I could do that lecture in my sleep. It was time for something new.

One way to keep your teaching fresh and invigorated across a career is to change—always try new things: new textbooks, new strategies, new assignments, new questions. Sometimes you can recycle, bring something back after a break, but you always need to be on the lookout for new ideas, new approaches, and new challenges.

And this not only is true for your courses but ought to characterize your teaching activities in a larger sense. Team teaching is a wonderful way to refresh and stimulate your instructional blood. It does not happen all that much at the present moment because of its cost, but consider inviting or exchanging with a fellow faculty member for a week or even for a guest lecture. Not only will this put your content in a fresh perspective, but if you truly share instructional responsibilities, you will see firsthand how somebody else handles the teaching tasks.

To sum up, there is much to be learned about teaching, and like so much other learning, this requires hard work but provides intellectual stimulation and a sense of personal accomplishment. Once you finally understand how and why an instructional strategy works, finally get the bugs out of an assignment, or at last find some group work that enables students to truly teach one another, you will have your decision to teach reconfirmed. So let the adventure begin!

Enthusiasm as an ingredient of effective instruction is both simple and complex. It begins and ends with concrete actions that transform the abstract attitude into visible manifestations. Most of the actions are easily implementable. You begin "to be" enthusiastic by doing them. But the moment you do, the complexities of this component emerge. The actions unaccompanied by genuine feeling lack integrity and compromise credibility. To make feelings explicit takes courage and involves risks. Our nervousness shows. We must work to control it. Enthusiasm is not permanently acquired. Its presence or absence is influenced by a host of factors, most notably institutional policies and practices. It must be cultivated, and we must work to sustain it. By comparison, other components, such as preparation and organization, are more straightforward and carry less emotional baggage. But no other component has the power to personally satisfy us and motivate students like enthusiasm does.

Background Reading

Ericksen, S. F. (1984). *The essence of good teaching*. San Francisco: Jossey-Bass. (Particularly chapter 12, "Sustaining good teaching over time.")

Palmer, P. J. (1990, January-February). Good teaching: A matter of living the mystery. *Change*, pp. 11-16.

Penner, J. G. (1984). *Why many college teachers cannot lecture: How to avoid communication breakdown in the classroom*. Springfield, IL: Charles C. Thomas.

Tompkins, J. (1990). Pedagogy of the distressed. *College English, 52*(6), 653-660.

3 | Preparation and Organization

As with other ingredients of effective instruction, evidence of preparation and organization is not established by announcement. Rather it is seen more tangibly in things like course materials. The syllabus, for example, can show that the teacher has clearly identified objectives, carefully designed the learning activities or assignments, and systematically developed relevant classroom policies and procedures.

Course-planning activities are useful in a discussion of this component of effective instruction. Using the syllabus as our focus, we will identify a set of necessary decisions to be made about course objectives and content, learning activities, and classroom policies and procedures. Besides revealing tangible evidence of a carefully planned and clearly structured course, the syllabus also communicates implicit messages about course tone and style.

However, as central as the syllabus is in establishing the preparation and organization of a course, it cannot be expected to do the job by itself. Students need more. What the syllabus sets in place needs to be supported by various presentation strategies that on a daily basis put course content and activities into a larger context.

Identifying Objectives and Deciding Course Content

Syllabus as Contract

Think of the course syllabus as a contract that spells out the terms of an agreement between you and the students with respect to certain learning outcomes. It's not a legally binding document, but it does advance the cause of accurate expectations, which many students in college are missing these days.

The first step in planning a course and preparing a syllabus is to identify the outcomes. What do you want students to know and be able to do at the conclusion of the course? This is no simple task. Most faculty underestimate its importance— their first thought relates to material and how much they could or should include in the course.

You should think of course objectives in light of the course description, which usually identifies general topic areas and probably already exists in the college catalog or departmental materials, provided it is an already existing course. If the course has not been taught previously, you may need to rough out a description; but at this point the focus should be on what students will learn and be able to do at the end of the course. Content needs to be thought of as the means that will accomplish learning outcomes, not as the end.

If writing out objectives seems unappealing, maybe these two alternatives will be more inspiring. Imagine you meet a student 5 years after having taken your course: What would you like the student to remember at that point? Or, clarify course objectives by constructing the final exam (at this juncture you may ignore certain realities, like class size, and design the perfect final). To design course objectives from this final, just imagine the skills and knowledge a student would need to perform well on that final.

Both the course objectives and description should be included on the syllabus. They usually are, but they are often stated perfunctorily and antiseptically. Remember, the syllabus is being written for the students, not the curriculum committee. Compare and contrast the following two examples. From an introductory-level animal science course:

The biology of animals that provide food and fiber for mankind. The composition, nutritional value, and factors influencing the composition of meat, milk, eggs, and wool are discussed initially. Discussions that follow are based on homeostasis, digestion, nutrition, feeds and feeding, growth, reproduction, egg laying, lactation, genetics, selection and breeding, and animal behavior. Laboratory sessions include the use of milk, wool, eggs, meat, rats, mice, chicks, calves, pigs, and chickens to demonstrate biological concepts discussed in lecture.

From an introductory-level political science course on American public policy:

This course seeks to provide you with analytical tools and practice in using them in order to enhance your ability to understand public policy as it unfolds throughout your lifetime. It rests on the assumption that virtually every facet of your life will be affected profoundly by the content of public policy and that the unprecedented challenges to the survival of humans on the planet will lead to massive disruptions in our "way of life" that will force everyone to become very concerned about public policy. Politics counts. Like it or not, public policy will be relevant to you.

The course will be divided roughly into two parts. The first, from the beginning of the semester to spring break, will present a set of analytical tools needed to understand the policy process and will describe in general terms some basic operating characteristics of the policy process. In the second half of the semester, we will acquire practice in applying the concepts and knowledge covered during the first half by examining a number of specific policies. You will learn something about each, but the ultimate goal is to help you develop a general way of looking at public policy that you can use to understand any issue.

The first lists course topics. The second relates the content to students—tells them in a clear and explicit way how and why they will be involved with the material of the course. It might be faulted for a fuzzy description of course topics, but it certainly conveys a persuasive message about the course. The point: Don't compromise the integrity of the course, but do recognize that students unfamiliar with the content and new to learning at the college level may need to be told explicitly how captivating and valuable a course experience can be.

With the course description and objectives established, content decisions are next. It is best to start with a general list of topics, maybe those in the course description. Textbook tables of contents or syllabi from faculty who have taught the course may also be useful. Assembling the list of topics raises the difficult issue of how much content.

New college teachers frequently err on the side of including too much content. A number of factors contribute to this mistake. First, new faculty certainly do not want to start off by teaching Mickey Mouse courses, and one way to avoid that is to be sure the course contains plenty of rigorous, complicated material. Second, new teachers often have a number of years between their undergraduate experience and their first teaching positions. The entry-level material we once stumbled over now looks easy and obvious. Even if it is not immediately familiar, it certainly does not look difficult. Finally, new teachers often succumb to the need to teach everything they know about the subject. We are usually not at our most confident when we first start teaching. We worry that students will not find us credible and competent. Having lots of content in our lecture notes helps to assuage those fears. However, it usually overwhelms our students.

To help make realistic content decisions, I recommend careful study of syllabi and conversations with others who have taught the course. In addition, spending time developing the course calendar helps to put content decisions into perspective. The more specific you are, the more valuable this planning activity will be. List all the class periods. Remember that some will be taken up by exams and discussions of exam results, possibly review sessions, discussions of homework, and student presentations. How many periods will you have to present material? How much time during these periods will students need to raise questions, discuss, apply, and/or practice the material? Obviously those are not easy questions to answer when you are new to a course. The answers become a bit clearer after you have been through the course several times, but the course content issue never gets settled permanently. But a calendar can provide some benchmarks that make a manageable list of course topics a more likely outcome.

At some point you will need to put the course calendar on the syllabus. Since you should consider adding exam dates, reading/homework assignments, and other deadlines, which you probably have not yet determined, now may not be the best time. But including on the syllabus a list of topics and the order in which they will be presented conveys a sense of structure and direction. Students, particularly first- and second-year students, benefit from having a course outline.

You should not worry if the course calendar "evolves" as your planning activities continue or even after the course gets underway. Label it "tentative" or "proposed," and tell students it may change. Yes, you can change it too much, thereby defeating this tangible sign of preparation and organization. But you can make necessary adjustments. In summary, the course calendar serves two purposes: It forces you to think through and make content decisions, and it gives students the chance to see the separate topics of the course in relation to one another. Activities completed during this sequence of the planning process will encourage you to make decisions in three important areas: course objectives as a means of determining what students should know and be able to do; course content in terms of how, what, and how much; and the course calendar as a vehicle to arrange and sequence content.

Designing Learning Activities

As important as decisions about objectives and content are, equally significant are the whole set of choices that pertain to the design of learning activities, a term that includes all kinds of student work, such as exams, homework problems, reading assignments, written work, projects, and presentations. Students do not learn in the presence of content per se. The teacher plans and organizes a series of systematic encounters—assignments. Their importance is documented by the fact that students spend 85% of their waking hours outside the classroom and most of what they learn they learn there—not in class.

We give students assignments for two reasons: first, to promote learning and second, to provide measures of their mastery of the material. Frequently, the second reason overshadows the first. We (that includes students *and* faculty) are all more grade oriented than we should be. We think about exams and assignments in terms of their grade-generating potential—forgetting their absolutely fundamental purpose: They promote learning.

For two reasons, decisions about learning activities need to be made before the course begins. First, they should be a part of the total course design. Our key organizational question—what students should know and be able to do at the conclusion of a course—applies to decisions about assignments, too. The kind and amount of learning activities introduced in a course directly impacts what students will learn and be able to do, just as course content decisions do. The second reason to make these decisions a part of course preparation activities is an even more pragmatic one: Students want to know about them—they will ask you early on, probably on the first day.

What are the key questions that should be answered about learning activities as one prepares and organizes the course? Most of them relate to the frequency, timing, and sequence of assignments. How often should they occur? Research argues in favor of frequent encounters with the content and against a single midterm, final, term paper, or course-long project. The frequency is particularly important for beginning college students. They need feedback about their performance early in a course—not necessarily grades but feedback. Often they come to college with inaccurate expectations. The earlier they find out whether their work measures up and what they can do if it doesn't, the better.

The frequency of learning activities, particularly the graded ones, needs to be weighed against your time commitments as well. The more assignments, the greater your grading burden. You don't want to give so many assignments that by the middle of the course all you are doing is grading them. You would be far better off giving fewer assignments and providing more complete feedback. I mention this because idealism and optimism often infects new teachers and becomes manifest in decisions about the number of assignments. All that said, for the sake of the students, if you are going to make a mistake, err on the side of too many assignments.

A simple but frequently overlooked issue related to timing has to do with when students have assignments due in other courses. Much as we might wish, ours is not the only course students are taking. In a 15-week semester many faculty give three exams, spaced evenly across the course. During week 5 then, a student may have three, even four major exams scheduled. That is a pressure cooker situation that more than likely results in compromised performance on at least one, if not more, of the exams.

Decisions about the sequence or order of assignments also need to be made. Should you start small and work up to more complicated ones? Bette Erickson and Diane Strommer (1991) recommend this method in their book on teaching freshmen. They say that term papers, for example, may be overly complex for beginning students. In entry-level courses a series of shorter papers allows more opportunities for students to practice and for faculty to provide them with feedback they can use in subsequent assignments. Students will also have more chances to develop their time management skills. The same sort of argument might be made about group work. Students, particularly beginning ones, will probably benefit from starting with smaller group tasks and working up to the more complicated ones.

One of the assumptions underlying this move from simple to complex, which is particularly relevant to students considered at-risk, relates to the need to empower rather than overwhelm them. Many students who come to college to-day are not especially confident learners. They tend to give up easily, before they should. Psychologist Raymond Perry (1991) has spent more than a decade studying how student perceptions of their abilities to succeed in college courses can be modified by different kinds of feedback. His work supports a fascinating conclusion: What students believe about their abilities to succeed has more impact on their success than the effectiveness of their instructor (as measured by student ratings) (see also Perry & Penner, 1990). Teachers are in a powerful position to affect what students believe about their abilities.

The timing and order of assignments in upper-division courses is important for a different reason. Here, students need to develop their abilities to assess their own work and to make decisions about tasks independent of teacher direction and control. They also need to apply, synthesize, and evaluate content. At this level you can and should let students make some decisions about their learning activities. For example, some faculty let students set their own due dates for course work. Others let them make decisions about the sequence of assignments.

Without deciding the kind and combination of learning activities you want to use, it is difficult to make decisions about the frequency, timing, and sequence of these activities. If you want to think further about it now, you may want to skip to Chapter 6 where I discuss assignments in the context of using them to assess student learning.

Classroom Policies and Procedures

Still another set of planning issues pertains to the actual conduct of the classroom. You can let these evolve as the class gets under way, but having made some decisions up front about grading, attendance, academic integrity, and classroom management reveals evidence of your preparation and organization and makes for a smoother functioning classroom. Grading is probably the area that comes to mind first and foremost. You do need to decide on a grading policy, and it does need to appear on the syllabus. Information on grading is discussed in the context of assessing student learning in Chapter 6.

Attendance

Are you going to require attendance? Take roll every day? Enforce some penalty for absences? Is there such a thing as an "excused" absence? How would you define it? Is there a limit on the number of these absences? What about students who miss exams? Will you offer makeups?

I wish I could offer the definitive policy. Unfortunately it does not exist. Faculty opinion and practice in this arena varies tremendously. The subject has not been researched in anything more than a token way, although faculty wisdom comes down hard on the side of student presence in class correlating positively with overall course performance.

The mistake I think faculty make in thinking about attendance policies is to get fixated on the details. Recently, I overheard two faculty members arguing with some feeling over whether there ought to be three or four excused absences per 15-week course. Conversations like that trivialize the real issue. We have attendance policies because we believe students need to be in class, and we are willing to try to "force" them to be there. This means we believe faculty have some role and/or responsibility in the learning of students. A much richer discussion would focus on the nature of that role and responsibility. Does it change depending on whether students are freshmen or seniors? Does it change depending on course content? Does it change depending on the instructor's need for control?

As with so many seemingly simple instructional issues, this one rarely gets settled once and for all. If someone collected the various attendance policies off my syllabi from over the years, I suspect I could be diagnosed schizophrenic. When I began teaching in the early 1970s I was still motivated by the spirit of the 1960s and had no attendance policy; in my heart I think I still subscribe to that notion. If a student can learn and do what I have decided she or he ought to be able to at the conclusion of the course without ever coming to class, what right to I have to "muscle" them in? Memories of some of my own college classes have still not faded. There attendance policies benefited the instructors whose fragile egos did not handle well playing to a half-full house.

What I learned during those early years, when I only taught beginning students, was that many of them mistakenly believed that they in fact could miss class and do well in the course. Most of them failed, needlessly to my way of thinking, and I felt a certain responsibility for that. So, I crafted a policy that did not punish those who skipped but rewarded those who attended. On 10 unannounced days I would take roll and give to all present a specified number of bonus points. I still like and use that approach for some of my courses.

But I discovered even that policy did not bring to class on a regular basis students who could really benefit from being there. By the time the eighties rolled around I was requiring attendance. Be there, no excuses. But sometimes students miss class for legitimate reasons—sometimes institutionally sanctioned reasons. I found it hard in terms of a policy to articulate the legitimate from the not legitimate excuses. Some students talk a very good line. An accident with Aunt Suzy's cousin Maude's toe can sound like a truly life-threatening family emergency. Moreover, with this policy, when they came to the office, we ended up not in intellectually rich exchanges over course material but in heated debates over whether or not an excuse was legitimate. So, I opted for the common practice of three unexcused absences before certain penalties start to kick in. What disturbs me is that virtually all students take all three. It is not a perfect solution.

I do not share my story with attendance policies because it is particularly seminal or insightful, but I think it is typical of the kind of evolutionary processes most of us go through as we try and try again to create the best possible learning experiences for our students. Our agonizing in the long run is healthy, but that does not make it pleasant or your planning tasks easy.

Academic Integrity

Most of the time our focus is on preventing cheating. Sometimes our policies repeat verbatim the institutional policy. Other times they make reference to it. In most cases the offense is discussed in terms of its punishment. We all know how seriously cheating compromises all aspects of our academic endeavors, but do our students understand? Perhaps we ought to cast the focus on prevention in terms of the need to promote the honest, ethical advance of knowledge.

Along the same lines, we need our definitions to be clear and explicit. Some researchers (among them Barnett and Dalton, 1981) have given lists of actions to faculty and students, asking them to mark those they considered cheating. The faculty and student lists disagreed considerably.

Classroom Management Issues

I'd put in this category a whole variety of student and faculty actions that impact on creating and sustaining a climate for learning. What about lateness—as in coming to class late, as in turning in an assignment late? What about leaving early? What about talking while the teacher or other students are talking? What about eating in class? What about sleeping or doing homework for another class during the lecture?

One of the reasons most of us opt to teach at the college level is because we do not wish to deal with precisely these kinds of issues. Unfortunately, disruptive student actions are a grim fact of life even at the college level. Rather than whine about their impropriety, we need to think about policies and practices as we plan, prepare, and organize the course. There are also differences between high school and college that make it much easier to deal with disruptions constructively. Students are not required to attend college. They are no longer children and as young (or not so young) adults, they can and should be made accountable for their actions. Said another way: Treat them like children and expect them to act that way. Treat them like adults and expect to see the corresponding mature responses.

For example, I have in my files a course syllabus that says in capital letters on page 2, "I SHOOT STUDENTS WHO COME TO CLASS LATE." The faculty member still teaches, so apparently he's either a bad shot or does not make good on his threat. A policy like this demeans students, however, and it makes being late a larger and more important issue than it deserves to be. I feel the same way about professors who handle the problem by locking the door at two minutes past the hour, leaving students to knock, beat, or otherwise disrupt the class in their attempts to get in.

Bear in mind you cannot with any policy or procedure "force" a student to arrive in class on time. The more you try, the more it ends up being a contest of wills that the student can win. Yes, you can "punish" students by penalizing their grades, but is that ethical? And, what if the student doesn't care about grades?

We are taking the example to the extreme. Students do get to most classes on time. You reinforce that norm when *you* arrive in class on time and do something important during those first few minutes of class. Institute some logical consequence or price to pay for being late. In one math class I observed, the homework problems appeared on an overhead screen as students arrived and remained there for the first three minutes of class. Then they were taken down and not put up again. The few late arrivers had to go down to the instructor after class and ask to see the transparency so they could copy the assignment. That is not a terrible "punishment," but neither is the crime.

Now, if you are teaching in a room where the only entrance is directly behind you and late arrivals can be enormously distracting to you and the rest of the class, I think you have to be firm. And in most cases an announcement will have the desired effect. Most students will respect and understand your request. They will comply, especially if you return to them the same respect and understanding. For example, tie a promise to end on time to an expectation that they arrive on time.

Your experience will help you learn which of these classroom management policies and practices you need to include on the syllabus. In the beginning, thinking through classroom climate issues as part of the planning process may be more important than articulating them on the syllabus. In the interest of not making mountains out of molehills, I would run the risk of too few policies on the syllabus rather than too many.

A Syllabus's Silent Messages

Our exploration of the preparation and organization component of effective instruction has focused on the syllabus as a document where our decisions about objectives, content, assignments, and policies can be stated to the benefit of the planning process and our students. The syllabus serves one other function related to several of the components of effective instruction. It contains silent, nonverbal, unstated messages about the course and instructor. Those messages will be conveyed either with or without your attempts to influence them.

One year, in my graduate course on college teaching, I gave students syllabi from various courses on which I had removed all the identifying information. I asked them to look at the language, tone, and style of each syllabus, as well as the kind of material each included, and then to conjecture how well organized each instructor was, how authoritarian, how student-centered, how enthusiastic, and so on.

Students wrote with anger about a syllabus that emphasized correct spelling but that contained typos. They saw this as an example of a double standard—one that applied to students while exempting the instructor. They rated instructors low on preparation and organization if no course calendar appeared or if it was largely incomplete. They equated syllabi that contained numerous classroom management policies with authoritarian professors who lacked confidence in their abilities to deal with students. Obviously we cannot stereotype or even make broad generalizations about instructors from these observations, but the match between the students' comments and my experiences in these classes certainly gave me pause.

If you are open to influencing these silent messages, you might consider using the syllabus to convey your enthusiasm for teaching and for the course. It can also reveal something about you as a human being. I'm thinking of one syllabus attachment I thought was particularly clever. The instructor, a quiet, reserved, senior faculty member, had constructed a one-page Dewar's scotch portrait-ad. It featured a xeroxed picture of him in an appropriately scholarly pose. He listed his heroes, latest novel read, most recent accomplishment, last vacation destination, number of years teaching, and his favorite scotch (which wasn't Dewar's). He never mentioned the document in class, but students often made comments about it in their course evaluations.

I'm not advocating this particular strategy for everyone. Part of its success derives, I think, from how well it fits this instructor. He is not a warm, friendly, effusive professor who is at ease talking about himself in class. But this is a man who in his own way cares deeply and sincerely about the teaching-learning enterprise. He is proud to be a teacher, and his portrait somehow attests to that.

I know another professor who ends a syllabus by wishing students success in the course and then personally signs each

copy. I have another in my file that the instructor has illustrated. If using the syllabus in this way fits comfortably with
who you are and the kind of relationship you aspire to
establish with your students, think creatively and innovatively about using the syllabus to convey your enthusiasm,
concern, and commitment as well as your preparation and
organization.

So far, the focus has been on course-planning activities as
a means of conveying your preparation. You should extend
the same kind of careful, systematic, thoughtful planning to
your daily preparation for classes. You should have objectives for each class—what students should know and be able
to do at the end of any given period. The content included
should be selected because it will help to accomplish those
objectives. Learning activities should be designed that enhance
student-content interaction. And everything we've said about
what the syllabus can accomplish applies to handouts you
might use on a daily basis.

Communicating Structure

Carefully preparing course material forces you to organize
the course. However, what these materials can accomplish
must be supported and further illustrated by the way material is presented in class. Said another way, you must communicate your structure. You increase your ability to do that by
understanding and acting on the differences between written
and spoken language and by using outlines.

Writing and Speaking: The Distinctions

The problem stems from the fact that organization within
the written and spoken realms is conveyed in different ways.
When you read a passage, something as simple as the period
at the end of the sentence signals the end of an idea. A new

paragraph hails a collection of ideas and information somehow separate and distinct from what has proceeded.

In verbal communication, the same sort of cues exist, but they are not "standardized"—there is no such thing as a paragraph gesture. You can convey a change in thought or the transition to a new idea by physically moving to a different location. You can remain stationary and signal the shift with a long pause or a repeated verbalization, like "Okay" or "Are there any questions?" Or you can provide verbal cues: "I've finished that area and am ready to move on to the next one." Without providing these markers your organization becomes tough to follow.

Understanding this simple but important distinction enables you to make conscious choices about how you will move across points and between ideas. Will you pause, gesture, change location, write the new point on the board/overhead, change speech speed or pitch? Using a variety of approaches and combinations will add interest to your teaching style, making it easier for students to stay with you for the entire period.

In addition to the less standardized organizational cues, spoken language also has less permanence than written language. If you are reading a passage and find yourself confused, you can retrace your steps, following the development of an idea across several paragraphs. The structure is fixed in the text. With the spoken word, you hear it once and it's gone. If a student's mind is wandering and you make the transition to a new idea, the student misses it. Or if your transition is a muddled one, students do not have the opportunity to hear it again, to pause over it and analyze what has happened.

For this reason, it may be useful to consider some modest exaggerations of the structural cues you use. I have a friend who is downright blatant. He will pause, put his fingers to his head as if he's pulling the idea out, and then say something like, "Here's something we haven't talked about before—something you need to get in your notes." I'm not sure you need to be that explicit in upper-division courses, but it does help in those content-dense introductory ones.

Using Outlines

You can provide students with the structure of a class period via some sort of outline. It might be a handout distributed as the class begins, or it might be shown on an overhead transparency. Or it might not be shared with students but used only by you to keep on track. Some faculty go so far as to duplicate their lecture notes and distribute them to students. They reason that if students are not trying to figure out which are main and which are supporting points, they will be free to focus on understanding the ideas. The case against this position exists in a fairly impressive body of research (Carrier, 1983), which identifies both a product and process value to note-taking. Said without the jargon, students benefit by leaving class with a set of notes, a product, but they also learn during the process of actually writing things down.

So what criteria helps you determine how to use outlines to communicate structure? I suggest the decision should be a function of the complexity of the content and your teaching style. If the content is dense with lots of new vocabulary, sharing an outline with students helps prevent information overload and makes it easier to focus on the content itself. Providing students with an outline also enables you to get through the material more quickly. This is particularly true if you are using diagrams or charts. It is time-consuming for you to draw those and for students to try to replicate them in their notes. You can preserve the "process" benefit of note-taking by providing the graphic but having students attach the labels.

How you use outlines is also to some degree a function of your own style. How organized are you? I am not at all. My office looks like somebody turned on a large fan and let it run unattended for some time. My teaching strengths relate to my spontaneity, my ability to detect an ounce of student interest and to parlay that into something much larger. I'm a teacher who goes with the flow, senses where the class is, and tries with varying degrees of success to bring content to that place.

Spontaneity and structure do not have a particularly compatible marriage. On good days, what interests students is one of the day's main topics. On others they may respond to a point that is not even on my outline. So, I end up getting sidetracked and although I may have the class's attention and involvement, I often end up teaching topics I never intended to bring up. A skeleton outline keeps me honest. I put mine on the side of the board at the beginning of the period. I make public statements about it and force myself to shut down whatever is happening in class 10 minutes before the period is over. We spend the remaining time going over the outline. What did we discuss? What have we missed? What else have we talked about, and does it relate to anything on the outline or in our readings? This method fits my need for spontaneity, my students' need for structure, and the fairly flexible nature of my content. It has made the marriage more compatible.

As you experiment with different ways and means of communicating structure, be sure to get feedback on their effectiveness from students. For example, during a couple of minutes at the end of the period, suggest they review their notes and underline several key ideas. Then ask them for some examples of what they have underlined. If they are all underlining your supporting material as opposed to the key points, you may need to try some other methods of communicating structure.

Early in my career a colleague suggested another useful form of feedback. Ask a student who is listening and taking notes in class if you may take a look at those notes. You can do the same thing a little more surreptitiously by looking at students' notes when they bring them in to discuss course content with you. For me it was a sobering experience. The student notes and my notes bore little resemblance to each other. One thing I noted, which all sorts of research has documented, is that virtually everything I wrote on the board ended up in student notes; and I was certainly not as circumspect as I should have been with regard to what ended up on the board.

Finally, when it comes to communicating structure do not neglect a simple rule that applies to all public presentations. They *all* need to have three parts: an introduction, a body, and a conclusion. You would be surprised how many lectures are delivered minus an introduction and conclusion. Your introduction should accomplish two purposes: It should capture the audience's interest and overview what is to come. The conclusion summarizes, distills, and synthesizes what has proceeded. In classrooms it should be longer than a minute and needs to be delivered *before* the period has ended. Speech teachers will tell you that the introduction and conclusion are the most carefully prepared parts of a successful presentation.

In this chapter, we have focused on the preparation and organizational tasks associated with teaching. We have addressed preparatory tasks in the context of course planning because few new teachers escape tasks associated with preparing for courses not taught previously. We considered organization from a presentational context because most often the relationships between pieces of content are established verbally.

Background Reading

Altman, H. B., & Cashin, W. E. (1992). Writing a syllabus. *IDEA Paper No. 27*. Manhattan, KS: Center for Faculty Evaluation and Development, Kansas State University.

Nuss, E. M. (1984). Academic integrity: Comparing faculty and student attitudes. *College Teaching, 33*(3), 140-144.

Stark, J. S., Lowther, M. A., Ryan, M. P., Bomotti, S. S., Genthon, M., & Haven, C. L. *Reflections on course planning: Faculty and students consider influences and goals.* Ann Arbor: National Center on Research to Improve Postsecondary Teaching and Learning, University of Michigan.

4 | Stimulating Student Thought and Interest

You hear a lot of complaints about students these days, but one is repeated more often and with more intensity than any of the rest. Students are passive. You see it from the first day as they sprawl back and recline in chairs they wish were lazy-boy recliners. The attitude is clear. "Okay, prof. Here I am. Do it unto me and points for you if it's pleasant and painless." Most faculty attribute these student attitudes to long years of being entertained by TV. It is probably more complicated than that and more directly related to the kinds of educational experiences students have had previously.

Regardless of the origins of the problem, faculty complaints have been substantiated by a number of prestigious and now frequently referenced national reports. In most of our classes, the intellectually curious, independently motivated, eager student is not in the majority. Is this a student problem? Many faculty believe it is. They will tell you it is not our job to motivate students. We are paid to teach the material. But most of us have discovered how frustrating and depressing it is to teach a group passive, disinterested students. So for our own sakes, we get involved in efforts to stimulate and motivate students and then end up worrying whether these efforts at "entertainment" compromise the integrity of a fundamentally intellectual endeavor. The same national reports that document widespread student passivity make an equally clear and compelling case for student involvement in learning, or active learning. When students are learning actively, they learn more, retain it longer, can apply it better and continue learning. The research basis for this case is made most convincingly in the ASHE-ERIC Research Report on active learning (Bonwell & Eison, 1991). Faculty may begin efforts to involve students in order to make teaching a more palatable proposition, but in the end it is students who benefit most, which puts efforts to entertain in a different context.

As a component of effective instruction, the ability to stimulate student thought and interest depends on a wide-ranging collection of strategies and techniques that fall under the active learning rubric. When student learning is active, according to Schomberg (1988), it involves acquiring and interpreting (or transforming) information. Strategies as common and familiar as questioning and as novel and innovative as learning communities all aspire to achieve student involvement and participation in learning. I propose that we broadly survey a range of active learning strategies that include questioning techniques, discussion, in- and out-of-class group work, and some examples of collaborative learning approaches. We will consider each in terms of its effectiveness to stimulate student thought and interest. With a clearer understanding of the strategies used to involve students, we will be in a better position to sort through the ethical issues related to a teacher's responsibility to motivate students.

Questions: Do They Make Students Think?

As an instructional practice, questioning may be the most common, widely used, and universally accepted instructional strategy. And therein lies the problem. It is too much taken for granted and too much used without insight or conscious awareness. Questions can make students think and they can stimulate interest, but the four affirmations that follow are qualified. These "Yes—ifs" propose that some ways of using questions are more effective than others if the goal is to motivate students.

Yes—If You Give Them Time to Think

Teacher wait-time, as it is called in the research, has been studied extensively in the K-12 arena and the findings agree. Most teachers wait less than five seconds, which is not long enough. Some research (Rowe, 1983) and most observation in almost any classroom confirms that college teachers are not any different. Student thought and interest is stimulated during the interval after the question is asked and before the answer is given. Five seconds or less does not allow much time for reflection.

You maximize the impact of that interval by lingering over the question, maybe repeating it, or maybe adding some commentary, "What do you think? It's an important question." I like to wander around the room when there's a question in the air. I look directly at the students, occasionally smile and finally, after what seems like an eternity to them and me, solicit the answer from a volunteer or call on someone.

I've observed faculty who use other strategies. One has students write key questions in their notes. "Here's a question you need to have in your notes." Another has students jot down ideas before the answer is discussed. If it is a question with two sides, some faculty poll the class. "How many think this is the answer?" "How many disagree?"

As a strategy to stimulate thought, questioning depends to a large degree on our ability to tolerate silence. And some of us do not tolerate it well. The press of material yet to present weighs heavy, and so we abruptly terminate the power of the question by answering it ourselves. Students note when this happens. Their predilection to passivity is rewarded—so they sit tight and wait. Pretty soon they get the "right" answer from the person who knows the content best.

All teachers, even very experienced ones, worry about prolonged silence in response to their questions. The most effective cure involves preventing the disease. Our actions must unquestionably demonstrate the sincerity of our efforts to get students involved. Consider two concrete suggestions. _First, establish an interactive norm early in the course._ I do not recommend waiting until three weeks into the course when students have some content under their belts and can answer knowledgeably before soliciting answers. If you plan to use questioning to get students involved in the course, you need to establish that norm early in the class.

Second, do not contradict verbal messages with nonverbal actions. Would you interrupt with a question if the professor regularly looked at her watch, made comments about how much material was still left to cover, and waited until the last two minutes of the period before formally asking, "Are there any questions?" You must back your claim of interest in questions with action, particularly at the beginning of a course. I have on occasion left a question unanswered when no one responded, telling the class to write the question down, think about it overnight, and expect that we will tackle it again the next day in class. Follow-through is important with this strategy. Remember you are attempting to disprove a common student experience: rhetoric about the importance of questions but a classroom reality in which few exchanges occur.

Yes—If You Don't Intimidate Students

As new teachers, it is hard to imagine ourselves as intimidating. But to students we sometimes are—often in the context of asking and answering questions. Faculty who intimidate students usually do not do it verbally. We are not given to calling answers "stupid" or publicly berating a student for a poor performance. More often, we "put students down" (an interesting metaphor) with a facial expression, by turning our backs on them, by our tone of voice, or by ignoring their contributions.

Sometimes we are even well intentioned. We hear something that is not really correct or something we do not follow, and rather than dealing with the answer and risking a put-down, we say politely, "Hmmm, interesting idea. Somebody else?" And if the next answer is not much improved, we respond, "Hmmm, interesting idea. Somebody else?" until finally we hear an answer we can deal with and then we respond. We are polite, but the fact remains that we have not dealt meaningfully with a contribution; that's a put-down in and of itself.

In addition to nonverbal put-downs, we can intimidate students by the way we use a strategy, for example, calling on students. When faculty discuss calling on students usually the focus is on whether or not we should. Like so many other instructional strategies, this one is not inherently right or wrong. It can be either. Students are intimidated when you stand over and glower down at them. An anonymous and impersonal address is also intimidating: "You in the blue shirt. No, not that blue shirt. The blue shirt with glasses." Students are also intimidated when you call on them and then deal harshly with their answers or if you use an authoritarian, aggressive style. On the other side, calling on students is not intimidating if you do it regularly, if you call on students by name, and if, occasionally, you let them off the hook when they do not know the answer or are unprepared.

In sum, when you ask and students answer, you stimulate thought and interest by really listening to their responses. Do not use the time to organize your notes, check the time, or turn to the next passage you need in the text. When you visibly value and use student contributions, you run little risk of intimidating them.

Yes—If You Handle Wrong Answers Constructively

Constructive responses to wrong answers are characterized by strategies like these three. First, *always focus on the answer and never on the student.* "There are some problems with that answer. It ignores some of the historical issues we talked about in class yesterday." The answer is wrong, not the student. It is a small distinction, but for students heavily vested in their own work and words, it is an important differentiation.

Second, *see if the mistake has been made by others.* That gives the student some company and you the opportunity to clear up the misunderstanding of several students. I heard an interesting twist on this approach in a math class once. A student gave an answer and followed up with an explanation of how it was derived to which the instructor replied, "The answer is wrong, but I'm glad you made the mistake. It's a common one and now I can show everybody how to avoid the error."

Finally, *help students to understand that we all make mistakes.* Leona Welch (1991) wrote in an article in the newsletter on teaching that I edit, "My classroom is a mistake-making place." In other words, everybody makes them and everybody realizes that mistakes often teach more than right answers. Students need to see that learning involves failure, trial and error, and a lot of false starts.

In this regard I think of a colleague of mine who taught agronomy for many years. He used to talk with his students about a "dumb" farmer he knew—a well-meaning fellow who lost his tomato crop because he planted it in soil that percolated poorly, overfertilized his alfalfa, and made several other egregious errors. He used to laugh openly and mock the "dumb" farmer until some of his students objected. Then he would announce to the class (with glee barely concealed) that since some had taken issue with those comments, he had decided to settle the matter once and for all. Tomorrow he would bring the "dumb" farmer to class and students could decide for themselves. The next day he arrived in class dressed in bib overalls and sporting a John Deere cap.

Our detailed discussion of wrong answers should not be taken to imply that responses to right answers are unimportant. They are just easier to execute. Perhaps our problem with right answers is that we do not make the most of this important opportunity to provide students with positive feedback. We stimulate further thought and interest by acknowledging good answers. Again, focus on the answer, not the individual. It is a good answer because it incorporates several ideas from the reading, it applies two theorems in deriving the solution to the problem, and so forth.

Yes—If You Get Them Responding to One Another

Often in a question-and-answer sequence, the student involved is the only one whose thought and interest is being stimulated. Once a student breaks the interval of silence with a response, everyone else feels they are off the hook. You see them relax. Most put their pencils down, look around, check the time, yawn, and generally take a short break. Once you resume the lecturing mode, they start listening again. How can you get them to attend to the comments of one another?

As already suggested, you need to model the behavior by listening carefully, but you may need to do more. In one of my classes something happened quite by accident that now I conspire to make happen. A student made a comment that was for me a completely new idea—something I had never thought of before. I did not know how to respond, but I knew I wanted to. So, I said to the student, "Gee, that really is an interesting idea. I have never heard or read that answer. I need to think about what you've said. Let me jot myself a note and I'll get back to you tomorrow." I moved back to the podium, took up my pencil and wrote the note. The class was abuzz. People were looking at each other's notes and asking, "What did she say?" It provided a perfect opportunity for me to point out to the class that not all the new, good, and important ideas came from the front of the room.

I have seen faculty use other strategies that effectively involve students in one another's responses. One makes notes on the board as the student comments. If the student is proposing some sort of explanation, the faculty member labels it "Susan's Theory" and may make verbal references to it throughout the remainder of the period. Another credits students from previous courses. "A guy named Bill who took this class a couple of years ago came up with a really good mnemonic for remembering these gas laws."

The most obvious way of getting students involved in the questions and answers of classmates is to let them answer one another's questions and/or comment on one another's answers. In far too many classrooms, you would think there was a law that stated that every student comment must be followed a faculty response of equal if not longer length. No such law exists nor should one. When we talk less, students talk more.

To conclude: Do questions stimulate student thought and interest? Yes—provided you give them time to think, do not intimidate them, handle wrong answers constructively, and get them responding to one another. For the new teacher this means time devoted to planning questions, to thinking about how students might answer and how responses might be fielded. It also means monitoring questioning strategies in class, becoming aware of when one breaks for questions and what kind of questions best fit the content. It means being aware of when students ask questions, what kinds of questions they ask, and how they respond to the answers given.

Not unlike enthusiasm, questioning appears deceptively simple. In reality the necessary skills are sophisticated and complex. The more work done on skills in this arena, the more work there seems to be. It is the occasional sequence that really works, that turns on intellectual lightbulbs on all around the room that keeps all of us trying.

Discussions

When students start responding to their classmates' questions and comments, the line differentiating questioning and discussion blurs. However, once the dialogue between students is sustained, a discussion occurs. Faculty (old and new) struggle with answers to three questions that are key if discussion is to stimulate student thought and interest and promote learning: (1) How do you lead and guide a discussion without controlling and directing it? (2) How do you get students involved in *quality* exchanges as opposed to conversations where their collective ignorance is pooled? (3) How do you give structure and closure to discussions?

How to Lead and Guide but Not Control and Direct

As an instructional method, discussion stimulates student thought and interest by promoting individual discovery. As ideas are exchanged, refined, polished and processed, conclusions emerge. They are the "discoveries" of those who have participated in the discussion, and even though time could be saved by offering the same conclusions up front, the process of having derived their own conclusions benefits the learners. The downside is that discussions often sidetrack, get bogged down in irrelevancies, and leave participants bored or frustrated. To be effective, discussions need to be led or guided, and most often this task falls to the teacher.

The trick is to provide the guidance while still preserving the opportunity for discovery and self-learning. Because students are passive and because good discussions require mental effort, students want faculty to do more than guide. They like "right" answers from the expert. If they do not state that desire explicitly, they convey the same message with their behaviors. During the discussion, they listen and write down what the teacher says but not what any other student says. They may ask the teacher question but never a fellow participant.

When the discussion flounders, the teacher often feels compelled to intervene, and so a vicious circle evolves: more teacher direction and guidance, less student involvement, more teacher talk, even less student talk and pretty soon it has crossed the line back to questioning and maybe even clear back to lecturing.

Faculty can break the cycle of control and direction with four strategies. To begin, *the teacher must make a commitment to discussion* and go to class determined to have a discussion. This states the obvious, but often students wear us down. We need to be firm in our commitment to this instructional strategy and willing to put up with some student frustration and discontent. Second, *teachers facilitate discussion by removing themselves from positions of authority in the classroom.* It is very hard not to control a discussion when you occupy the position of power at the front of a room with students seated in rows. Students will communicate directly with you if yours is the only face they see. They will direct comments to you if you control the flow of conversation by calling on people. If at all possible, get students seated so that they can see and hear each other. Sit with them and let the group regulate the flow of conversation.

Next, *leading a discussion includes providing some sort of structure, framework, or context for the discussion.* Before the discussion begins, you need to think about the issues and conclusions you want to emerge in the discussion. Then you need to spend time figuring out ways to get those conclusions and issues to emerge. Often we try to raise issues or direct the way to conclusions by asking questions. Too many times they are poorly prepared questions that end up illustrating the proverbial notion that the quality of the questions determines the quality of the answers. Clear, cogent, well-sequenced questions are not prepared on the spot.

Finally, *good discussion leaders attend to the process.* They keep track of where the discussion has been, where it is now, and where it appears to be headed. They can tell if it's leading up a blind alley, if people are repeating ideas and nothing new is emerging, or if a group has sidetracked. The discussion may be animated but not on topic. Good leaders intervene at both these points—not necessarily with criticism but by changing the group's direction. They may identify a comment that moves the group to a side street off the alley. Or they may refer back to one of the questions with which the discussion began using a recent comment. The goal of the guidance is always the same: It helps the group to find its way.

How to Have Quality Exchanges

In addition to requiring some sophisticated leadership, successful discussions need to promote quality, intellectual exchanges among students. Frequently this does not happen and students complain. They object to having paid precious tuition dollars to hear the comments of fellow students who share their ignorance. The challenge to the teacher then is ensuring the intellectual integrity of discussions. How do we accomplish that?

The answers are easy but often difficult to implement. First, we need get the message across to students that discussion is an activity for which they must prepare. The beginning of the course is the best time to establish this norm. And here as well, actions speak louder than words. You can tell students all you want that they must prepare for discussion, but if they come unprepared and discuss without any negative consequences, they have proven beyond debate that they do not have to come prepared. Consider strategies that contain consequences. Several faculty members I know assign different readings to different groups of students. In class students are then convened in new groups in which each student has completed a different reading; then the groups are given a series of questions to answer that integrate the ideas from the separate readings. If a student is not prepared, his or her peers are affected by that lack of preparation.

Second, do not underestimate your own power as a role model. You need to embrace discussion techniques with enthusiasm and conduct those class sessions with obviously high expectations. Granted this may involve some play acting. You know in your heart-of-hearts that students are probably not well prepared and eager to exchange ideas. But you conduct the class assuming they have read the material and have issues they want to discuss. Be obviously disappointed when they don't, but carry on. Be relentless, cajole, encourage —smile, relax, and wait patiently knowing that an important point will be made shortly. Yes, you are performing and you will need to do that in ways that preserve your integrity and that of the educational enterprise—but never underestimate the power of your expectations to influence student performance. Expect them to be great and they will be. If you doubt, promise yourself you will see the movie *Stand and Deliver*.

Third, the intellectual quality of discussion improves to the extent to which students are taught how to discuss. I suggest using discussion incrementally, working students up to longer and more complex discussions. Especially with beginning students, start with short discussions (say, 10 or 15 minutes) and less complicated outcomes. The quality of a class discussion can be improved if you begin by letting students first talk about the topic among themselves. Some faculty call these "minidiscussions." The discussion question or topic is introduced and students are asked to share initial opinions or thoughts about relevant facts from previous class sessions with two or three other students sitting nearby. The discussion begins with several individuals reporting on the focus of those minidiscussions.

Last, but not least, some instructors dramatize their reaction to poor quality discussions. If their attempts to launch a discussion engenders little or no student response, they may abruptly dismiss the class, saying they do not intend to present a lecture on this material and that if students want to learn it, they must come prepared to discuss it.

How to Provide Structure and Closure

In most cases, discussion structures itself inductively. A variety of isolated comments, topics, and questions lead (sometimes not too directly) to some larger conclusion or context. However, these conclusions may not be evident or obvious to students who are frustrated by the seeming randomness of a discussion. What should they put in their notes? They need some sense of structure and closure.

You can make students aware of the structural issues associated with discussion by devoting a bit of class time to a discussion of discussions—how they work and how students can learn the most from them. Often we let a discussion go on too long before we take a crack at summarizing and looking for structure. Try taking short breaks during the discussion during which you and the students jot down key points, unanswered questions, and relevant information.

In these high-tech days, my teaching took a low-tech turn after I read a wonderful article by Reloy Garcia (1991), "Twelve Ways of Looking at a Blackboard." He proposes a variety of useful ways to use the blackboard to summarize, focus, and structure discussions. He suggests that teachers track the discussion on the board:

> Perhaps because it poses no threat to the student, the blackboard helps to shift the burden of the discussion to students. Partly this is because the teacher is working for them, helping to record or shape their observations. What students think and say, the blackboard attests, is worth a public record. (p. 5)

Discussions need to conclude before the period does. In the remaining moments, closure can be provided in a number of different ways. Give students a chance to either make some notes or review those they have made. Two or three overarching questions can help students organize what they have written down. On occasion (usually Friday afternoons of football weekends) I have been known to ask students to review, add to their notes, *and* write one test question they think they might ask about the material. Most of the questions are not very good, but occasionally one shows promise. If you ever use any of those questions on an exam, you will have them for life. They will take the activity seriously—in fact, I have even had classes who asked if they could propose questions.

I observed one faculty member who finished discussion by comparing the class summary (in this case, a listing of four key ideas) with his own summary that he had prepared before class. One of the issues on his list did not emerge in the class discussion. He directed students to material relevant to it and proposed that they consider it during their own study time. One of his points he deferred to one made by the class. He indicated that he thought the class point was more on target than his own. A strategy like this can be very empowering to students.

Sometimes I think faculty avoid these kind of explicit closure activities because they are hard. Summarizing and giving structure to a discussion that covered a variety of issues and included the voices of many different students are not easy. It requires intense listening and sophisticated synthesizing skills. The skills develop over time and with conscientious self-monitoring— and lots of trial and error.

A good discussion continues in the hall after class or during study time as students continue to ponder the issues and test the conclusions. It motivates by empowering students to take on the content and make it their own. It is a powerful teaching tool but not one that achieves its goals accidently. Just as a good syllabus reflects careful planning, so does a stimulating class discussion.

Group Work

The distinction between group work and discussion is blurred. If a discussion involves a small number of participants it may be called group work. In any group work, discussion is the major means of communication. Like discussion, group work is successful when instructors prepare and pay close attention to a variety of small but important details. Like discussion, group work is successful because it forces students to actively process and apply information. It also teaches some important skills of cooperation. Group work typically occurs in two arenas: activities completed in class and group work that occupies students outside of class. In each arena, several key decisions need to be made before the group work begins.

In-Class Group Work

Size of the group. Most of us can relate to frustrating group experiences where size prevented the efficient operation of the group. The majority of those who have written about groups recommend keeping the group size small—say five to seven members. Some even recommend smaller numbers. In small groups, the pressure to participate makes it difficult for any member to be noncontributing. If the group needs to make a decision, odd-numbered groups can decide by voting.

Composition of the group. Should you let students form groups themselves or should you create the groups? It depends. If it is early in the course and the group activity is a short one, it is much more efficient to let students form themselves into groups. If some groups have five members, some seven, some more female than male participants, it will not matter if they are interacting for only 20 minutes. However, if the interaction is to be a sustained one, variables like these and others may be significant. In larger classes, groups provide a wonderful opportunity for students to meet each other. That happens when group membership changes.

There are lots of ways of organizing and getting students into groups. You need to avoid the scenario where 10 minutes of the 20-minute group activity time is consumed by forming groups and finding places for them to meet. You need to get that organized before, not during, class. If the room has chairs bolted in rows, encourage the groups to use the space however they wish. Let them sit on the floor if they want to, or let them stand up. Chairs in rows are a barrier to group interaction, but students are often creative in overcoming obstacles.

Nature of the task. For in-class group work, the best advice is to keep the task simple and make it absolutely clear. Groups can spend inordinate amounts of time trying to figure out what they are supposed to do: Witness any number of faculty committees. The goal is to get the group focused on the task itself. So, ask for three reasons for x based on the assigned reading, or instruct the group to take and justify a position. I recommend giving the task to them in writing or having it on a transparency so that it can be consulted regularly by the group. You might also consider the kind of task you give groups from a developmental perspective, with simpler tasks offered in the beginning and more sophisticated ones near the end of the course.

Amount of time on a task. There is no magic formula. We do not know that groups are more productive, active, or personally satisfying if they interact for 20 minutes as opposed to 15 minutes. The key here is the relationship between the task and the amount of time assigned to it. In the beginning, make a guess and then solicit feedback from students as to whether they had enough time to complete the task. Often faculty err on the side of too much time when they first start using groups. If the time limit is a bit tight, regularly apprising the class as to the amount of time left encourages groups to be more task oriented. All groups need some time to socialize, but a class has a variety of opportunities to fill that need.

Use of group products. The most important decision to make here is the decision to do something with what the groups produce. Nobody likes to devote time and energy to a group task and then have the group's product (be it a report, statement, position, answer) ignored. With in-class group work, the products can be used in many ways. You can have the groups report back. If the class is large and the groups are small, 10 group reports are likely to bore everyone. Have some groups report and then give groups not reporting an opportunity to add or comment on the other groups' conclusions. You can have groups submit some sort of short paper or possibly complete a form that solicits ideas and information. You can grade these, although it would probably be more useful to somehow summarize what the groups concluded and use that information in a subsequent class session.

For an example that illustrates the broad range of tasks groups can complete and a creative way of using a group product, consider an instructor who tells students she is planning to spend the next period reviewing and summarizing materials that will be included on the upcoming exam. She asks the groups to identify the topics and questions they would like to have her address in the review session. Not only is this a task tailor-made to stimulate student thought and interest, but their recommendations provide her with some excellent feedback as to the topics they consider the most important and/or the most confusing.

Out-of-Class Group Work

Size of the group. The advice pertaining to groups convening outside of class is pretty much the same. Keep the group size small. Students are busy people and a large group may be unable to find a common meeting time. If you are teaching a large proportion of commuter students, recognize the difficulties and inconveniences associated with out-of-class meetings. In these cases you may need to let groups meet during the class sometimes, and you will need to design tasks that can be easily partitioned so some of the work can be completed independently, thereby necessitating fewer group meetings.

Composition of the group. If the group will be meeting regularly across the course and preparing a product that will be graded, it is probably best for the instructor to assign students to groups. Membership can be balanced in terms of ability, gender, ethnicity, possibly major, and any other relevant criteria. Thomas Muller (1989) reports a creative way of composing groups that involves identifying particular skills and background experiences that are relevant to completion of the project he assigns groups. He designs a survey to solicit information from students about the skills and experiences they bring to class. He uses the information on the survey to construct groups, spreading students with relevant skills and experiences across the groups.

Nature of the task. The sky may well be the limit. Faculty use groups to evaluate promotional campaigns or a set of programs possibly offered by some group on campus; to prepare video programs, perhaps demonstrating a process or promoting something, such as safety; to interview and hire key personnel in a fabricated company setting; to develop ad campaigns; to make a product; to review and make recommendations about course texts; to run experiments; to write a report; or to complete computer stimulations. For new faculty interested in course-long group projects, it is wise to consult with faculty in the discipline to get ideas and see how different group projects are designed and graded. I would recommend that group-work novices start with simpler projects and work up to more complicated ones as their experience grows.

Time spent on task. The amount of time very much depends on the nature of the task. In the beginning you cannot do much more than make a guess. Seeking advice and feedback from students completing group projects will help you make better estimates.

Use of group products. Most often faculty grade the products of out-of-class work groups. Sometimes they can be shared with the rest of the class, although if all groups do presentations, large amounts of class time can be consumed and some of the presentations may be of marginal quality. Some faculty have all group presentations videotaped and then share the best tapes or live performances with the class. Some give groups the options of presenting their findings orally or in a written report.

Grading group work offers its own set of challenges. How do you make sure that students get grades that reflect the amount and quality of their contribution to the group? Unless you observe the meetings of each group, you are not in a good position to assess the contributions of individual members. Some faculty resolve the dilemma by splitting the group grade in half. The first grade is assigned to the product, and everyone in the group gets that grade. The other grade is an individual's peer evaluation completed by group members, who may do something like assign both a rating and a ranking to the contributions of other members. In my experience, students often object to having to grade their peers, but I consider it a valuable experience and one that approximates a fairly common professional practice.

How to manage group processes. With stable group membership and interaction across a number of weeks, the possibility of negative group dynamics certainly exists. Some faculty take a fairly hard line when this occurs. They point out that groups who become counterproductive in professional arenas either figure out how to overcome their problems or live with the consequences of being dysfunctional. By this logic, even negative experience can teach students a great deal, but it is not particularly enjoyable learning.

Others are less hard-nosed and more committed to teaching students something about effective group processes. These faculty may spend time in class talking about how groups work, may share written information describing constructive contributions to groups, or they may meet occasionally with groups to discuss process-related issues. One faculty member I know has each group appoint a liaison who meets intermittently with the teacher and the other groups' liaisons to discuss process problems, like members not carrying their weight. They brainstorm solutions and report on progress with previously identified problems.

One final note on a different kind of out-of-class group work: Do not overlook the potential of study groups. Again, faculty use them in all sorts of different ways to accomplish a variety of purposes. In large classes where students frequently do not know each other, the option of being part of a study group can personalize the experience as well as provide needed study support. Some faculty help organize study groups for students who have difficulty in the course and enlist the services of some of the better students as study group leaders. In addition to facilitating study groups, some faculty have better students prepare study materials, guides, questions, problem sets, or sample essays. There should be some sort of reward for students who spend time supporting the study efforts of others, such as extra credit or the possibility of being exempted from an exam.

In some cases the use of study groups is less optional and more systematic. Donald Keyworth (1989) reports that he assembles study groups and then lets them take a group exam. Students complete an individual exam first and then in their study groups prepare a group exam that represents their collective wisdom on the questions. If the group score is higher than the individual score, the individual score is upped by a certain number of bonus points. Keyworth reports, "As I've observed groups working together on their common answer sheet, I've been very encouraged by the depth of analysis which this process stimulates in almost every group."

Because many students learn better when they work with others and because these skills of cooperation are so needed by our society and the world, study groups as well as group work experiences in and out of class ought be part of a teacher's instructional repertoire. However, they are discussed here because they are particularly effective ways to promote active learning.

Collaborative Learning

Collaborative learning experiences are special types of group experiences. Studied much more extensively in terms of their effects on learning at the K-12 grade level, these approaches to group work are now being used and studied much more extensively in the postsecondary arena. Although the field is still struggling with definitions and not all the researchers and practitioners agree, in one of the few articles that tackle definitional issues, Barbara Leigh Smith and Jean MacGregor (1992) propose that collaborative learning is the "umbrella term" under which six different groups of strategies can be considered. They maintain that all these educational approaches involve "joint intellectual effort by students, or students and teachers together" to the end of "mutually searching for understanding, solutions, or meanings or creating a product" (p. 10).

Six collaborative learning approaches are identified by these two authors and are briefly highlighted here. Cooperative learning "structures small group learning around precisely defined tasks or problems" (p. 10). Students work together cooperatively, but individual accountability is retained. Problem-centered instruction aims to develop problem-solving abilities, help students understand complex relationships, and learn how to make decisions in the face of uncertainty.

In undergraduate education, writing groups (used in a variety of courses besides English) are the most widespread collaborative strategy in use. This strategy involves students working in small groups at every stage of the writing process, from brainstorming topics to editing final drafts. A variety of peer-teaching strategies also employ collaborative learning approaches in that they put students (generally more experienced ones) in the teaching role. When discussion, as we have described and discussed it, occurs in the context of small groups, Smith and MacGregor consider it a collaborative approach.

Some of the most interesting uses of collaborative learning involve creating learning communities. Most of these approaches involve an "intentional reconfiguration of the curriculum" (p. 18). In programs like freshmen interest groups, linked or cluster courses, or a coordinated studies curriculum, a cohort of students (usually beginning ones) take a series of courses together. In the Freshmen Interest Groups, in addition to being in three courses together, students have a one-credit course with a facilitator during which they explore the interconnections and relationships among the courses in which they are enrolled. Both linked and cluster courses as well as coordinated studies programs involve faculty in the cross-course collaboration. In linked courses, for example, students may take a political science and English course with overlapping and interrelated assignments. Coordinated studies programs often involve thematic courses where the perspectives of several different disciplines are brought to bear on the topic.

Synthesis Courses

As a new faculty person, you may not have time to implement collaborative learning approaches that require major curriculum revision, but it is important that you be aware of them and recognize a widespread interest in collaborative learning approaches as the vehicle to involve passive students who need to have both their thinking and interest stimulated.

Effective use of questioning, discussion, group work, and collaborative approaches stimulates student thought and interest. This component of effective instruction, like preparation and organization, relies on a set of concrete, acquirable skills. You can learn how to positively affect student motivation. At this level the teaching tasks are relatively straightforward—not easy or simple but clear. However, at the point where we apply our knowledge, where we put into practice what we have proposed in the chapter, a whole series of less tangible and more perplexing issues come into play.

To Stimulate and Motivate: To Entertain?

We began the chapter by raising two related ethical issues. To what extent is it a faculty responsibility to stimulate student thought and interest? And, when do well-intentioned efforts to involve students cross the fine line and become "entertainment"? I don't have definitive answers to either of those questions. They are complicated queries and, in large measure, situationally dependent. What I can propose are some general principles or guidelines and leave to you to sort through the details that pertain to you.

As to whether teachers have the responsibility to motivate students, it may be that our responsibility is to *try* to motivate and involve students—to labor, as we will discuss in the next chapter, to find relevant examples, to seek to relate our content to their needs and concerns, and to use regularly and systematically the active learning strategies described in this chapter. But is that enough? My good friend who teaches agronomy assumes for himself a larger responsibility. He thinks of it in terms of the old adage, "You can lead a horse to water but you can't make it drink." In this case the horse is the student and the water is learning and the larger role involves "putting salt in the oats so that when the horse gets to the water, it's damn thirsty."

I like the metaphor, but I haven't yet figured out how to derive generalizations or operating principles from it. What it does more effectively is raise yet another complex set of issues that relate to the fact that teachers can use both intrinsic and extrinsic motivators. If you have unannounced pop quizzes to ensure that students keep up with the reading, you are "salting the oats." The problem is that while this may encourage drinking, students may end up hating the water. Overreliance on extrinsic motivators diminishes the power of intrinsic motivation. Pretty soon students are only doing the work because they have to, and just as soon as they don't have to, they won't. Think about it this way: If yours is the introductory sociology course, the only one that students in a variety of other majors have to take, you have one opportunity to acquaint them with this field. If that first encounter is an unpleasant one, that bodes poorly for future encounters with the subject. So, when "salting the oats" we need to do it with a delicate, not easily specified blend of intrinsic and extrinsic motivators.

It may be easier to work backward—to begin by looking at the policies and practices we use and see if we can derive from them a better understanding of the role we are assuming we have for student learning. As we noted in Chapter 3, a discussion of your attendance policy, if you have one, and the reasons for it will uncover some of the assumptions you are making about how students learn and the role you think teachers should take in changing student habits and orientations to learning. If you aspire to change how students approach learning, you are choosing to teach something more than just content. Most of us justify these incursions into noncontent arenas because we believe they facilitate student learning. Because experience and research have taught us that students who are frequently absent or who are uninvolved and passive in class do not learn as well, we take some responsibility by requiring them to come to class and making an effort to motivate them to learn. A guideline begins to emerge: Whatever role the teacher assumes, its legitimacy must be measured against student learning.

With the question of whether or not it's entertainment, the same guideline applies. I use anecdotes to illustrate, clarify, and distill points. My repertoire grows and changes as the years roll by, but I have my old standbys. For many years one of these was a lengthy story I used to tell about an ongoing disagreement my former spouse and I had over how to load the dishwasher. It was a stupid disagreement but served to beautifully illustrate a whole variety of negative conflict resolution strategies. I always told the story with relish, because it sort of vindicated my position and because students loved it. They laughed at all the right places, listened attentively, and I thought they better understood the concepts.

One day in class, several students in the front row chatted and smiled as we waited to begin. "We're really looking forward to class today," one of them acknowledged. Curious, I inquired as to why. "My roommate had this class last semester, and she said today's the day you tell the dishwasher story. She said it was the best story of the whole semester." I was a bit taken aback, pleased—but somehow uncomfortable. There was a question I had to ask. "Did your roommate say anything about the point of that story?" "Not really," the student replied, "but she did tell us some of the details."

I told the dishwasher story that day, but when I got back to my office I faced the hard fact. The dishwasher story had to go. It had become the point, rather than making the points. On those terms it was entertainment—motivating, even captivating, but it didn't help students learn.

The student learning guidelines make it easier to determine when it's entertainment. If what I do in class helps students to learn because it motivates, stimulates, involves, and intrigues them, then it's justified and appropriate. If whatever I do does not make the learning easier, better, or more long-lasting, it has no place in the classroom. There are some important implications in that statement. Many commonly accepted classroom practices that err on the side of too many boring lectures might have to go if we apply the principle in that direction.

Most of the time what motivates faculty to discuss the entertainment issue is not the role it does or does not play in student learning but their own discomfort with this "performance" dimension of teaching. Many of us find it hard to envision ourselves doing a Johnny Carson or Joan Rivers routine, coming to class in costumes, or dancing before students as some of our more dramatic colleagues have been known to do. But the question here is really one of degree. There are lots of steps on the way to becoming a Carson or Rivers. Most of us have hardly taken more than a step or two in that direction. We don't err on the side of too much entertaining. We err more often on the side of boring.

Another guideline that should help sort through and operationalize these issues involves the very premise of this chapter. Effective instructors stimulate student thought and interest. We are trying to encourage cerebral activity—to make people think. It's that dual objective that helps maintain the appropriate balance. Our content helps us as well. In most of our fields, it is not light and relaxing, something to be experienced without much mental muscle. If something is going to be entertaining in class, it will more likely be us and not the material—that gives us more control. The amount of responsibility we have to stimulate student thought and interest and the determination of the legitimacy of our efforts both relate to maintaining the integrity of the educational enterprise. I have proposed that we use learning outcomes as the measuring stick against which our efforts are assessed.

We end where we began—with the need to overcome the passivity of all too many college students. We have proposed a variety of active learning strategies as the antidote. Implicit in our use of these techniques is the assumption that effective instructors successfully motivate and stimulate student thought and interest *and* that justification for these efforts ground themselves on more and better learning for students.

Background Reading

Billson, J. M. (1986). The college classroom as a small group: Some implications for teaching and learning. *Teaching Sociology, 14,* 143-151.

Garvin, J. (1991). Undue influence: Confessions from an uneasy discussion leader. In C. R. Christensen, D. A. Garvin, & A. Sweet (Eds.), *Education for judgment: The artistry of discussion leadership* (pp. 275-286). Boston: Harvard Business School Press.

Goodsell, A., Maher, M., & Tinto, V. (1992). *Collaborative learning: A sourcebook for higher education.* University Park, PA: National Center on Postsecondary Teaching, Learning, and Assessment, Penn State University.

Hyman, R. T. (1982). Questioning in the college classroom. *IDEA Paper No. 8.* Manhattan, KS: Center for Faculty Evaluation and Development, Kansas State University.

Welty, W. M. (1989, July-August). Discussion method teaching: How to make it work. *Change,* 41-49.

5 | Explaining Clearly

As a component of effective instruction, clarity tends to be more like enthusiasm and less like preparation and organization and the ability to motivate students. It is more difficult to identify the kind of concrete activities, strategies, and techniques that are included in Chapters 3 and 4. The ability to explain clearly seems less specific, and, like enthusiasm, the specifics alone belie a much greater complexity and interconnectedness.

Clear, effective instructors are simple enough to describe. They have the ability to ascertain when students are confused or not following and can at that point intervene in ways that diffuse the confusion and enlarge the understanding. Sometimes that intervention may involve crafting an alternative explanation that often has little in common with the first one offered. Sometimes even that second attempt to explain may fail and it will be followed by a third alternative. Sometimes it is the ability to take an idea apart, to separate it into component pieces, and then to show how those parts relate and add up to an integrated whole.

Effective instructors who are clear are particularly skilled at making the content relevant to students. They aid understanding by making esoteric, abstract, and seemingly irrelevant ideas, concepts, and information important to students. They manage to persuade students that there are reasons to know and become involved with the material. In this way the ability to explain clearly supports efforts to motivate students.

Part of making material relevant derives from the ability to select or construct examples that are meaningful to students. These examples serve to connect students and content. The examples are sometimes stunning bits of information (like an isolated statistic or powerful quotation); other times they are stories, metaphors and analogies, applications, or samples. At all times they make content compelling and serve to illustrate something larger.

As with the other components, a new teacher's ability to explain clearly develops over time, and one should begin teaching with realistic goals and in concrete arenas. I propose that the following three skills are at the heart of clarity and therefore are the best places to begin: the ability to ascertain when students do and do not understand, the ability to make content relevant, and the ability to construct, select, and use examples effectively.

How to Know When It Isn't Clear and They Don't Understand

It may seem as though the cart is being put before the horse on this point. If you explain clearly in the beginning, confusion would never result. True enough. Clear explanations derive most fundamentally from intimate and absolute understanding of the content and secondly from a thorough understanding of the learners before you. You will have to take care of your development in the first area. New teachers (and sometimes others who are not so new) frequently do not understand the learning needs of students and as a result students do not understand the instructor's explanations. So, we begin by exploring how to tell when the material is not clear to students.

The advice in this section can be summed in a nutshell—watch them, ask them, and listen to yourself. Students provide ample nonverbal cues when they are confused and will offer verbal feedback once they know you care. This advice is simple but it can be applied more effectively once it is understood more deeply.

The nonverbal cues are there if you look for them. Facial expressions can connote confusion and frustration and are often accompanied by sighs. Sometimes students look at one another to confirm that they are not the only lost souls. Sometimes they may look at each other's notes or talk quietly (on a good day) to see if they can discover the missing link.

You need to be aware of those nonverbal cues, although you should not rely on them exclusively. Nonverbal messages are by nature ambiguous and open to alternative interpretations. In the classroom in the midst of teaching, we are not in the best position to decode these messages. As we have already noted more than once, we have a vested interest in our teaching and that bias affects our ability to be objective observers. That objectivity is compromised further by the act of teaching itself. You have on your mind a million things, including listening to what you are saying at the moment, figuring out where you want to go next, being mindful of the time and the need to involve students, to name just a few at the top of the list. You cannot give the nonverbal feedback you are getting from students your full undivided attention.

So, if you sense their confusion, the best bet is to ask. Be careful how you word the query. Often it is best not personalized. "Bill, you looked confused—what's the problem?" puts Bill in the position of having to admit before a group of his peers that he has a problem. Better to make the query more general: "I sense that some of you aren't following. Where did I lose you?"

Response to the request may or may not confirm your feeling. You may have misread the signals and they are not confused. (The fact that signals can be misread means they can also be missed—so, you should sometimes ask even when you don't think they are confused.) Refer to material we explored at length in Chapter 4: Wait patiently for their questions and deal constructively with their responses. Asking whether or not there is confusion demonstrates the sincerity of your commitment to student understanding. From the student's perspective, it's potentially risky business admitting to the teacher that one is in the dark.

Sometimes you need to do more than the commonplace "Are there any questions?" Ask the questions to ascertain the degree of understanding. You can also encourage students to explain the material back to you or to other students.

In addition to watching for verbal expressions to determine degree of understanding or confusion, try soliciting some written expressions as well. Pat Cross and Tom Angelo (1988) in their work on classroom research propose a one-minute paper technique in which the teacher asks students at the end of the period to write down the one thing from that day's class they are most certain they understood and the one thing they feel they need to learn more about. Information like this provides teachers with immediate and relevant feedback. If something is not clear to a large number of students in class, more time can be devoted to it in the next class—or if class time is not available, students can be referred to a collection of key passages in the reading or problems that will provide more opportunity for practice.

Michael Strauss and Toby Fulwiler (1987) have reported on an innovative question-box technique they used in a 300-student, introductory-level chemistry course. At each of the classroom exits they placed a box labeled "Thoughts, Questions, Concerns, Critiques, and Commentary." Using a thermofax technique, the teachers transfer the student questions onto transparencies and devote the beginning of each class period to a discussion of them. They report, "We have found that when students write their own questions, they usually do so in simple, jargon-free language. This, we believe, promotes greater attention, better understanding and, consequently, improved learning. Noise levels in the classroom testify to this. You could hear a pin drop when we first put a transparency up" (p. 257).

Another way to figure out when material is not clear is to listen to your own explanations. All of us on occasion have been known to babble, ramble, wander, and in other ways offer a less than coherent explanation. If you feel yourself doing that, deal with it honestly. Students will respect you more, not less, if you acknowledge, "I don't think I made that very clear," "What I just said didn't make much sense," or "I'm having trouble figuring out where I'm going with this point." Admissions like these take courage, but they open windows and clear the air so that understanding is more likely to result.

In sum, if students are confused there will be nonverbal cues that you should watch for and inquire about. The teacher's responses to nonverbal, verbal, and written messages play a key role in getting students to be clear about what they do not understand. Combine these strategies with an honest acknowledgment of any failed explanations, and greater clarity in class is an almost sure consequence.

Making the Content Relevant

Inherently a part of the ability to explain, establishing the relevance of the content powers the student drive to learn. Much of what we teach students in college is not easy or particularly exciting. In most disciplines there is a considerable amount of groundwork to be laid before the more stimulating work of creating and expanding knowledge can occur. Students experience considerable frustration building those foundations if they are not shown the relevance and application of this initial content.

Part of the problem involves our own familiarity with the content. With countless hours of course credit behind us, the centrality of this initial learning is so obvious we forget how it appears independent of a larger contextual framework, and consequently we do not help students by explaining how this beginning knowledge relates to subsequent learning. But the lack of relevance goes in another direction as well. We often fail to relate what students are learning to their interests and concerns. The ability to do this rests squarely on our knowledge of those interests and concerns. When you start out as a young teacher this is not as much of a problem as it becomes as you get older and the traditional-age college students seem so much "younger." Even in the beginning it is important that you maintain contact with your students, chatting informally about what they consider important. That knowledge will enable you to connect the course content with their world.

I am reminded of a colleague who teaches in a remote, rural part of my state where unemployment is high and commitment to education low. He teaches philosophy and only uses primary sources. Students struggle with the reading. He begins many class discussions with a clipping from the local paper—some event that just beneath the surface entails ethical issues. He starts very low-key—"Anybody heard about this? What do you think? Why did the person commit this crime? Any details not mentioned in the paper that might be relevant? And what should happen as a consequence?" The discussion generally heats up. The community is small and people care. At the point when the class is particularly animated he quietly asks, "Why are we talking about this?" Students generally play along. "Oh, there's probably something in the reading about this." "What?" At first students don't know what, but gently and relentlessly he brings the current event to the ancient text. For students it becomes a game they play with enthusiasm.

It also helps students if you show them later in the course how something they learned earlier is being applied. This is easier in those fields where content is linear and new knowledge builds directly on what has been learned previously, but it can happen in all fields to varying degrees. Do not expect students to see all the connections. Remember they have only a limited frame of reference. This is their first or second course—you have how many by comparison?

Examples: The Case in Point That Makes It Clear

Examples provide a specific instance of the larger concept, idea, or principle. By understanding the case in point, maybe even several of them, students can generalize to the larger notion. Think of examples as windows that offer a view of the larger idea. Windows have borders. We only see part of the whole, but if we look through enough different windows, the view of what's out there becomes clearer.

For the teacher, examples can be thought of in terms of answers to three questions: (1) What are the characteristics of a good one? (2) How do you build a repertoire? and (3) Are there different kinds of examples?

As for the *characteristics*, I will defer to a simple but sound typology proposed by Stephen Yelon and Michael Massa (1987). Good examples have four elements: They are accurate, clear, attractive, and transferable. Accurate examples are "appropriate for the type of knowledge, should fit the idea to be taught, and should fit its purpose in the lesson" (p. 13). To enhance the clarity of an example, these authors propose "making the example concrete and brief, . . . including ideas known to the students, and . . . making the characteristics of the example apparent" (p. 14).

Attractive examples are ones that interest students. That is, they should relate to the experiences and aspirations of students. The attractiveness of an example is enhanced if it has certain novel aspects and is credible and realistic. The transferability of examples has to do with how they relate to one another and the need for them to range from easy to difficult and to represent varied situations and circumstances.

Most new teachers discover the importance of *building a repertoire* in the process of teaching. I still remember the flush of embarrassment I felt during my first year teaching when a student asked if I could provide an example to illustrate a point I was trying to make—I had none, and in that moment of need none came to me.

You can acquire examples in one of two ways: Construct your own or borrow from others. Both ways are legitimate. Often examples come to us, sometimes out of our own experiences and sometimes as a result of concerted thought. The characteristics we have just discussed provide a helpful criteria against which our own examples can be selected and constructed.

Good examples are to be found many places, including the writings, speeches, and conversations of others both inside and outside our fields and higher education. Sometimes good examples come from students—on occasion, in response to a request. I remember early in my career I experienced a great deal of difficulty trying to explain the literary concept of reification. The definition, "treating an abstraction as though it were concrete," never seemed to convey to students the sense of it. Red tape was the example that appeared in most of my texts. I used it but without much luck. Somewhat desperate, one day in class, I acknowledged, "I need a better example to make this idea clear." From the back of the room, a normally quiet student proposed, "How about the Statue of Liberty?" "Perfect!" Liberty is the abstraction and in this case it has been quite literally made concrete. I have used that example ever since and give Pete Randall credit. Borrowing examples from others does not imply being dishonest about where they came from. It is also important to note that examples keep. Yes, after years they can go stale, but that is not generally a problem during the first years of their use. With the press of everything else upon new teachers, sometimes it is easy to let good examples slip by. Often our notes for class focus on content and do not include examples. This leaves us with the task of reclaiming them the next time we teach the course. If you struggled to explain something in class and wished you had a good example, you should note that. One of my colleague affixes a Post-it note to her class notes after each period. She lists what worked well and the two or three parts of the session she would like to improve. Frequently she'll note: "Need better examples for *x*." Her technique also works well to add focus to the sometimes limited time we have to prepare for a class session.

When can you sit back and relax, knowing your repertoire of examples is large enough? Probably never. It is hard to imagine having too many or even enough examples. The large repertoire is not so much for use in class, although it is nice to be able to pick and choose, as it is to have lots when you need them. Students learn in different ways and you can never tell in any terribly predictable fashion what example is going to work for which student. You need lots at your disposal in case you reach an impasse.

As for the *kinds* of examples, consider four: stunning bits of information; stories; metaphors and analogies; and demonstrations, simulations, and case studies. The stunning bits of information are particularly memorable, notable, or compelling. They illustrate, in some senses prove, the existence of a larger problem. The statistic of the percentage of college content considered irrelevant or the 8,000 lectures to be delivered by the average professor are examples. Quotations also fall under this category.

Stories, real or fabricated, also aid attempts to explain clearly. Jakob Amstutz (1988) uses a vivid metaphor to describe what stories can contribute to efforts to explain.

> I tell a lot of stories. Stories are nails that I hammer into the wall. On those nails, I can hang up the whole, usually abstract, conceptual stuff of a philosophy course. If there are no nails in the wall, all the stuff falls down and will be forgotten. But if there are stories, illustrations, visualizations, they will not be forgotten; and contained in the stories there are the problems and the concepts. (p. 5)

Stories, if they recount one of your experiences or an experience about which you have firsthand knowledge, have the added advantage of letting you personalize the content. Through your stories students vicariously experience applications of course content. Those of you who come to academe after a career elsewhere will find that your "real-world" experiences add a special power to your teaching.

Stories, however, are not without liabilities. If they are particularly vivid and compelling and you tell them with a certain dramatic flair, it may be the story students remember and not the point the story serves to illustrate. If all your stories feature your exploits and conquests, you may acquire a somewhat unsavory reputation as the teacher who always tells war stories. Liabilities notwithstanding, the power of the illustration or case in point to offer insight into an abstract concept or idea should not be underestimated, and stories should be the kind of examples teachers look for and use.

Metaphors and analogies are also effective tools that aid efforts to make something clear. To say that the unknown is like something that is known is to build a bridge that links the familiar with the unfamiliar. Biology professor Allen B. Schlesinger (1986-1987) reports that he rarely attempts to explain a complex concept "head-on" in an introductory science course.

> My first effort is invariably the use of an analogy involving an example with which everyone is familiar. I never treat a concept such as potential energy as an abstraction and avoid using symbols at the outset. I start with concrete examples, water accumulated behind a dam, for instance and then develop some of the most obvious characteristics using that example. (p. 17)

Schlesinger does point out that metaphors and analogies can only go so far in creating understanding.

> Analogies are temporary scaffolds useful in the construction of a concept, but it is inaccurate to confuse the scaffold with

the building. The scaffold must be abandoned at some point. You cannot explain the world using analogies of the world. Sooner or later you must deal with the thing itself, not a portrayal of it. (pp. 17-18)

Demonstrations, simulations, and case studies, though different, can be considered together as a group of more extended and elaborate examples. They take time to prepare, to present, and to participate in but in exchange offer the opportunity to experience content in very close to real situations. Demonstrations, particularly easy to use in the sciences because of the observable nature of many of the phenomena being studied, provide an example of how what we may talk about in class and read about in text actually works.

Computer technology makes simulations a particularly powerful teaching tool in that a myriad of time-consuming calculations can be completed quickly so that the student can see a range of answers and options. Computer software can be used to show students the implications of a set of decisions, say, in the operations of a business. Programs in these fields interject new information at various points, which then require additional student decision making. If students work on simulation exercises in teams, the experience provides an example not only of content applications but of group dynamics.

Generally less showy than computer simulations, case studies offer the same sort of extended, real encounter with the content. Methods for using cases were developed in the business fields, but the approach has wide application and is used in a variety of professional education contexts. The case presents the story (sometimes real, sometimes fabricated) that unfolds into some sort of dilemma or problem. It ends without resolution, leaving the students to figure out the best solution or course of action. As with large-scale group projects, I would caution new faculty to move slowly into these areas of extended example. Resources available in a given field should be surveyed and the advice of faculty who have used these methods sought.

In this chapter we have tackled the somewhat elusive ability to explain clearly by proposing that new faculty begin developing skills by focusing efforts in three areas. First, and probably most fundamental, is the ability to ascertain when students do and do not understand. Another integral part of clarity is the ability to make the content relevant. When students understand the relevance of content, it becomes clear to them why they must learn it. Without that context and perspective, motivation suffers and learning falters. Finally, examples are an essential tool in efforts to explain.

Background Reading

Christensen, C. R. (1987). *Teaching and the case method: Texts, cases, and readings.* Boston: Harvard Business School Press.

Williams, W. C. (1985). Effective teaching: Gauging learning while teaching. *Journal of Higher Education, 56*(3), 320-337.

6 | Knowledge and Love of Content

In some ways, less can be said about this component of effective instruction than about the others. There is little help to give if you are missing knowledge and love of your content. You need to cultivate both. However, content incompetence is not a prevalent problem among college teachers. Jerry Gaff (1978) queried 1,642 college students as to needed improvements in college teaching. He gave them a list of 30 possible improvements and asked them to rank them in order of importance. Improving the content knowledge of the instructor was dead last on the list. Increasing instructor enthusiasm topped the list. Most college faculty know their content and are enormously attracted to it. They are not always as public as they should be about these academic love affairs, but the attachment is there and in Chapter 2 we proposed a variety of ways to that instructors can capitalize on it.

In this chapter I want to challenge several prevalent assumptions about content and its role in teaching. Assumption 1: More is always better when it comes to the amount of content in a course—and a corollary assumption: Covering content equals teaching material. Assumption 2: The most appropriate instructional orientation of faculty is to the content—witnessed by the statement, "I teach chemistry, political science, health education," or whatever, not "I teach students." Assumption 3: If you know it, you can teach it.

More Is Better When It Comes to Content

No self-respecting faculty member, new or experienced, wants to teach a Mickey Mouse course. If there is respect to be gained in teaching, it comes to those who teach rigorous courses, ones packed with plenty of dense, complicated content. Most of us struggle under the weight of too much content to cover. We are always behind, always trying to catch up, always feeling as though we are charging breathless to the course's finish.

Even a quick review of textbooks in most of our introductory courses confirms our preoccupation with content. These weighty tomes may be professionally impressive, but most students find them intimidating. A few years back Mary Budd Rowe (1983) did a fascinating content analysis of several entry-level, two-semester chemistry texts. She found that on the average those books introduced five new concepts a page and that the amount of new terminology contained in the book surpassed that presented in a first-semester foreign language course.

In fairness, the problem cannot be attributed exclusively to a sense of misplaced professional pride. Some of the increase in textbook size and course content is in response to the rapid growth of knowledge. In virtually every field there is more and more to teach. In spite of this, the length of courses is not on the rise and neither is the ability of most college students to handle more complicated content.

I do not propose any sort of compromising of academic standards, but I do suggest that we ask ourselves and our fields, When is there enough content in a course? How do we know? What criteria do we use? Answers to those questions are related to the corollary assumption that it is our primary job to cover content.

Faculty speak often about "covering" content. "I've got four more points to cover before the end of the period." "The next exam will cover chapters 6 through 10." "Do you cover self-efficacy in your intro psych course?" The use of this word is both interesting and incriminating. The bedspread covers the bed. Leaves cover the ground. They both conceal something beneath them. Is that the objective when we cover content? I once saw a great cartoon of a rotund faculty person who was teaching some sort of problem-solving class. The board was covered with problems and he was standing squarely in front of it. You could see bits of problems on both sides of him. The caption read, "Aim not to cover the content, but to uncover part of it."

Besides finding the word troubling, I am also concerned by the implicit assumption that if we have covered the content, our duty is done. You can cover all sorts of content, but that does not necessarily imply that you are teaching the material. I'm now reminded of a Peanuts cartoon in which Charlie Brown brags to a friend, "I taught Snoopy to whistle." His friend replies, "I don't hear him whistling." Charlie Brown points out, "I said I taught him. I didn't say he learned." Charlie Brown is right, sort of. Students are responsible for learning, but we shortchange their efforts when we see teaching only in terms of the transfer of information.

Finally, as motivated as we may be to cover more content, we simply cannot keep up with the growth of knowledge. Sometime in the not too distant future (maybe even now), we simply will be unable to teach students everything they need to know. In fact J. J. Lagowski (1985) calculated that at the rate at which knowledge is doubling in the field of chemistry, a chemist with a 35-year-long career will have to learn 80% of what she or he needs to know *after* having concluded their formal education.

Christopher Knapper and Arthur Cropley (1985) challenge the basic assumptions of undergraduate education proposing that rather than focusing on content, our first priority ought to be the development of learning skills that students can employ across their lifetimes. They do not propose content-free courses, such as one where we teach critical thinking, but they do encourage us to see content as the means to developing these skills, not the end in itself. Knapper (1988) explains the position:

> We are advocating the importance of people learning *from* life and *throughout* life. Obviously, this contrasts markedly with our traditional system of 'education by inoculation' in which students are given a sort of preventative dose of 15 years or so of education in the (false) hope that they will never have to bother with it again. (p. 1)

As a new faculty member, probably untenured, perhaps teaching part-time, you should respond to the preceding discussion of content quantity with some caution. I am challenging a prevailing assumption and one that cannot be addressed only on an individual level. I consulted once with a faculty member who taught in a beginning math sequence. He felt very strongly that there needed to be less material in the course. However a decision to eliminate three chapters from the syllabus would have been foolhardy. In early math courses, the content is linear, new knowledge builds on what has been laid down in earlier courses. Math 20 is predicated on the assumption that certain content has been taught in Math 10. In this case, the conversation about what and how much to include in the beginning course sequence needed to occur at the department level.

Hopefully this discussion has raised some questions about the assumption that more content is always better. The measure of a good course should not be exclusively or even predominately a function of how much material it contains. Students need to be challenged and the intellectual rigor of our courses must be preserved, but there are other ways of doing that besides cramming more content into courses. Now may be the time to return to Chapter 3 where we propose that time be spent articulating what a student should know and be able to do at the conclusion of a course. If an essential part of what a student needs to be able to do is to continue learning, maybe the emphasis ought to be on developing learning skills.

I Teach Chemistry, Political Science, Health, . . . Name Your Field

The problem with the orientation is that it excludes students. This is not a question of either/or. We need to strive for balance, and the current orientation of most faculty tips the scale decidedly toward the content. The imbalance should be no surprise. Our education develops expertise in our fields. We are not taught about students and how they learn.

In the very scant literature on how teaching skills develop, some hypothesize that there is a continuum that orients us to content on one end and to students on the other end. New faculty tend to start on the content side and as their teaching experience grows they become more student-centered in their teaching. The hypothesis follows common sense. It is difficult to get too taken up with the learning needs of students when you have never taught the material before. Your time is consumed by searching for examples, trying to anticipate student questions, and wondering whether you understand a concept well enough to explain it.

The focus may need to be on the content during those first teaching experiences, but there will come a time when struggles with the content will diminish. Many student questions you have heard before, the background reading you need to review is xeroxed and in the back of the lecture file, your transitions are smoothed out and/or the equation is fixed in your mind. At that point, you are ready to devote yourself to teaching students.

But their learning needs should be part of your orientation to teaching from the very beginning. You should know—and you probably do, even if only at an intuitive level—that students learn differently. We all do. For example, when you order something from Sears and have to assemble it, do you dump all the pieces out on the floor and go to work? Or, do you look for the instructions, review them, and assemble the object by following them?

Research on these learning styles has helped us categorize and better understand the differences between the ways individuals learn. Most of the effort has focused on the development of instruments that can be used to identify an individual's dominant learning style. At this point we have lots of different instruments that identify lots of different styles, most of which are related and overlap. We can say for certain that people approach learning tasks differently. We cannot say how many discrete learning styles exist.

To give you a flavor, let me highlight findings of David Kolb (1981) whose Learning Styles Inventory, based on a theory of experiential learning, identifies four major learning styles. A person who is a *converger* works best when there is a simple, correct answer to a problem and is at the opposite end of the continuum from the *diverger* who is happiest generating multiple ideas and solutions to a problem. *Assimilators* are good conceptual thinkers who like to integrate diverse items into solutions and are opposite from *accommodators* who learn from experience and experimentation using a hands-on approach.

The work of Kolb and others has a number of important implications for teachers. To allow students to benefit from being more aware of themselves as learners, you could do something as formal as administering one of the learning style inventories in class or something less formal, like having students write a short paper describing and reflecting on the success of the learning methods used to prepare for an exam.

A number of persons have hypothesized that teaching style somehow reflects an individual's learning style. The common sense substantiation for that assumption might be based on the approach many of us take when we design a course: We try to put together the kind of course we would like to take. Little research has addressed the relationship between teaching and learning style, but the new teacher would do well to analyze favorite instructional strategies and methods in terms of what they imply about preferred approaches to learning.

Most notably, this research prescribes regular variation in the methods used to present material to students and to assess their mastery of it. Said more bluntly: If you give a mid-term and a final, each having 75 multiple-choice items and that is the only vehicle used to assess student learning, you have made it more difficult for some students to do well in your course. Or, if you never visually represent any of the concepts in your lecture, you have made it more difficult for some students to comprehend the content.

In an excellent article Svinicki and Dixon (1987) explore in concrete, practical ways the instructional implications of the Kolb model. They propose different assignments that respond to the learning needs of four different styles and describe corresponding presentational strategies. For example, if you learn by observing, you will find that preparing logs and journals, participating in discussions and brainstorming sessions, and responding to questions effective ways to learn. We need more research that explores the instructional implications of the learning styles research, but until it emerges, faculty need to bear in mind the old adage "Variety is the spice of life."

Finally, with regard to learning styles, college teachers should be aware of another application emerging from this research. Kolb (1981) hypothesized and has proven that disciplines can be characterized as having a learning style. In other words, those of us in the humanities tend to be divergers while our colleagues in the natural sciences tend to be convergers. Kolb studied students whose learning styles were not matched with that of their disciplines and found that those students tended to transfer out of those fields; if they stayed they reported working more hours than their counterparts, tended to have lower GPAs, and were more likely to drop out of college. Although the implications here do pertain to the experiences of individual students, the large implications have to do with how we can open up our fields to new and innovative ways of knowing.

So as we teach content, we must be ever mindful that we teach it to students who will attempt to gain mastery of it in documentably different ways. Building on this general knowledge, we need to be particularly mindful of the learning needs of those students entering college who are considered to be at-risk. Students can be at risk of dropping out for a variety of reasons. Some lack prerequisite knowledge; many come to college poorly prepared. Some may need to combine work and school in order to pay for their education. Some may not have the necessary support systems at home or may lack motivation and drive. But the research has been very clear in documenting that many of the students who do leave our colleges and universities *are not* minus the mental muscle it takes to succeed.

To make matters worse, often these students who do drop out come from underrepresented groups (African Americans, Latino/Latina students, or women in male-dominated fields). These are the very students who most need to succeed in higher education if we are to redress the social inequalities that exist in this country.

Too often there is a kind of intellectual elitism that pervades the thinking in our disciplines. Extraordinarily difficult entry-level courses are believed justified so that students unable to cut the mustard get weeded out early. It is true that many students select fields of study for which they are poorly suited and that gaining self-knowledge is an important part of a college education. However, a discipline needs to carefully assess who is getting excluded—for instance, do students who are droppping out of a particular field belong to the same race or gender? At issue is not the compromise of academic standards. No one is proposing that disciplines credential anyone other than qualified, certifiably competent graduates, but many of us are proposing that the disciplines take as hard a look at the learning needs of students as they do at the content included in courses.

What instructional strategies and techniques contribute to the success of students at-risk? They need the same good teaching all students need. It is just that the presence of that quality instruction is much more pivotal in their success than the success of other students. Said simply and succinctly, they need to be actively involved in learning. Of all students, they are the ones least likely to succeed if they sit passively and are uninvolved in their classes. They also need to be empowered as learners. They need to have teachers who believe that they can succeed—teachers who help them develop an accurate understanding of what it takes to succeed, who believe they can go the distance, and who are willing to travel with them. Finally, they need frequent and constructive feedback —not just grades but commentary on all aspects of their performance and progress.

Teachers cannot do it alone. Institutions who are admitting students who are at-risk must make a real and significant investment in their success. They must provide resources and services to support what teachers are doing in class. The task is not an easy one, but the results have large and important implications for the decades ahead. Recognizing differences in learning styles and making a commitment to the learning needs of students are part of the recognition that teachers have a responsibility to both content *and* students.

If You Know It, You Can Teach It

The final assumption about content embodies the notion that excellent instruction is, in sum and substance, knowledge of the content. There are no dimensions to the teaching phenomenon that are not intrinsically a part of knowing the material you teach.

Like many proverbial notions, this one contains some truth. We know that content competence is *one* of the research-identified components of effective instruction. We have hypothesized it may in fact be the foundation upon which the other components build. However, it is not all that is necessary for instruction to be effective.

There are several problems embedded in this orientation to teaching. The first may well be the most significant. To say that teaching requires nothing more than knowledge of the content devalues the activity and contributes further to its already second-class status. As should be clear by now, **teaching is in fact a complex and complicated phenomenon whose variability and dynamic nature make it extremely difficult to understand and even harder to do well consistently.**

In modern times, colleges and universities with all sorts of different missions have grown increasingly infatuated with the research university model. Funds, prestige, reputation, and all sorts of institutional resources go to faculty who contribute to this research enterprise, much to the dismay of those committed to teaching. In the process, teaching has increasingly become an accepted, routine part of the professor's job. "Release time" is a coveted commodity at most institutions and it virtually always "releases" one from teaching obligations.

The teaching-versus-research debate is an old, tired, counterproductive one. For most institutions it cannot be an either/or proposition. Rather, room must be made for both as bona fide, legitimate, valued functions of the university. The issue is not how we devalue research, but how we better value teaching and broaden our definitions of scholarship as Ernest Boyer has proposed in *Scholarship Reconsidered* (1990). I submit that recognizing it as an intellectually rigorous activity, one that faculty need to practice with knowledge and awareness, values the teaching phenomenon. It is devalued by an orientation that oversimplifies its complexity by subsuming it in knowledge of the content.

A second problem with this orientation to teaching emerges when one considers how to improve. If effective teaching is a function of content competence, then ineffective teaching must be a problem of content incompetence. So, in a class where students talk among themselves, do not respond to questions, titter at the antics of other students, and generally come to class unprepared, problems are attributable to the instructor's lack of knowledge of the content and can be remedied if he or she spends more time mastering the stuff and substance of the course. The position we have taken throughout this book prescribes exactly the opposite. This teacher needs to learn more about teaching students and less about teaching content.

Those new to college teaching struggle in the beginning to master the content of their courses—as they should. But even as they do, they must that recognize that their first efforts should also focus on developing essential teaching skills. You must know your content, if you are to teach successfully, but you must know much else as well.

Our consideration of content competence as a component of effective instruction may seem to have downplayed its importance. Perhaps that is justified in light of the strong orientation to content our discussion has exposed. Most college teachers—even those new to the profession—know much more material than they can reasonably teach students during the average length of a course. From the beginning their work focuses on realizing several common assumptions that in fact compromise the effectiveness of their efforts to teach students.

Background Reading

Boyer, E. L. (1990). *Scholarship reconsidered: Priorities of the professoriate.* Princeton, NJ: The Princeton University Press.

Knapper, C. K., & Cropley, A. J. (1985). *Lifelong learning in higher education.* London: Croom Helm.

Svinicki, M. D., & Dixon, N. M. (1987). The Kolb model modified for classroom activities. *College Teaching, 35*(4), 141-146.

Weimer, M., Keehner, J., Parsley, K., & Wells, H. (1993). *Teaching students at-risk: An annotated bibliography for faculty.* University Park, PA: The National Center on Postsecondary Teaching, Learning, and Assessment, Penn State University.

7 | Assessing Their Learning and Your Teaching

Most do not know how to construct a valid test.

A book for first-time college teachers would not be complete without a chapter on grading. However, my chapter title reflects a larger, more inclusive perspective that ties grades to learning and learning to instructional quality.

Too often, the focus is on getting grades. Students frequently "grade grub," making every point or fraction worth a fight. They are this way because our society, including their parents, view grades and use grades as important stepping stones to successful careers. Students' preoccupation with grades forces us to develop elaborate and detailed grading systems. The focus on grades is appropriate so long as we see grades as a (that is, one) measure of learning. They are not an end in themselves but a reflection of something much more important: how much the student has learned.

What makes the focus on grades potentially risky is their inherent imprecision. They measure what is known at a moment, not what will be retained and used subsequently. They are only as valid and reliable as the instruments used to measure the learning. Most of us construct those instruments with little or no knowledge of test design. As a consequence, students sometimes get grades that *do not* reflect how much they have learned, which also makes the link betweens grades and learning tenuous.

This chapter is also predicated on the assumption that the assessment of student learning needs to be linked to the assessment of instructional effectiveness. The relationship is not a cause-effect one: x amount of good teaching does not necessarily equal x amount of student learning. There are intervening variables, such as student motivation and level of preparedness, over which the individual teacher has little direct control. Moreover, learning is a student responsibility. It is possible to teach extremely well, and still have students who fail. Teachers cannot learn the material for students, which means that at some point our responsibility is fulfilled independent of whether learning results. However, teaching that routinely produces little or no learning should be suspect.

There is a kind of intellectual elitism within the academy that denies the link between learning and teaching. It allows that an instructor who has given an exam that 70% of the class has failed or whose class average is 30 is not responsible for this extraordinary level of student failure. It is rather a case of students failing to meet course standards. A professor who stands tall in the doorway to the discipline is exonerated.

From the perspective that links learning and teaching, student failure would not be regarded so cavalierly. If a teacher believes he or she made a good faith effort to teach the material and still has a significant portion of the class failing, some warning should be sounded. (Of course, it can be a false alarm. It is possible for whole classes of students to be unmotivated, unprepared, and unable to meet course standards.)

But often students do poorly because they are being taught poorly. Poor performance of students in any class should stimulate self-assessment on the part of the teacher. Why are so many students failing? Is the content beyond them? Is that their fault? Is the pace too fast? Do the assignments poorly prepare them? Is the feedback given not resulting in improved performance?

Seeing the relationship between learning and teaching requires a high degree of professional ethics and intense but balanced personal honesty. If students are failing, one obvious solution is to ease up on the grading and consider the problem solved and the teaching successful. Or, the teacher inappropriately takes all the blame when in fact the students may have *chosen* to fail, despite the excellent instruction they received.

From this larger perspective that ties grades and instructional effectiveness to learning, we will consider nuts-and-bolts issues associated with developing and using exams, written work and projects, presentations and performances. For each, the links to learning will be made in terms of general principles, specific types of assessment activities, and feedback that improves performance.

Assessing Their Learning: Exams

We begin with exams, not because they are the most important, but because they are the most commonly used and misused assessment vehicle. As with other areas in this chapter and this book, we are covering a large, complex area briefly and at a very introductory level. A book in this series, *Tips for Improving Testing and Grading* by John Ory and Katherine Ryan (1993) treats the topic with the much greater detail it deserves.

The role exams play in efforts to assess student learning is highlighted by five general principles that integrate what we know about test construction, student learning, and notions of preparation and organization presented in Chapter 3.

❶ *Work for instructional congruency.* That's a fancy way of saying that what you emphasize in class, in the readings, and on homework problems should be emphasized on the exams. You put students in an impossible situation if you include one question from material

Content
validity

that you spent three days on in class but have four questions on a topic you introduced in the final 15 minutes of a period. If you opt for this approach, you do not encourage students to learn what is important but get them focused on trivia and trying to figure you out. Remember the key question from Chapter 3: What do you want students to know and be able to do at the conclusion of the course? Exams should be designed with that kind of learning in mind.

❷ *Be concerned about the reliability of the exam.* Exams are like bathroom scales—if the scale is out of adjustment, the measurement is inaccurate. If you write a multiple-choice item that is not clear in its intent, students will choose the wrong answer, not because they do not know the material, but because they cannot make sense of the question. A good exam is like a clean window. It's there, but it doesn't get in the way. It gives you a clear, undistorted view of what a student knows and can do.

❸ *Err on the side of frequency.* More exams are better than too few, particularly for entry-level students and populations considered at-risk. Most of those who study entry-level students counsel against one midterm and one final. After that, the advice is less specific and more dependent on your individual situation. There is probably a point at which exams become so frequent that they cannot really be considered exams. However, most faculty err on the side of too few as opposed to too many.

❹ *Match desired learning with exam type.* Multiple-choice exams are not inherently better or worse than essay exams, take-home tests, or matching questions. Each exam has assets and liabilities. Some achieve some learning objectives better than others. The decision of which ones or which combination to use should be the result of an attempt to match learning goals and question types.

❺ *Think about ways of making exams approximate reality.* Classroom testing situations tend to be very artificial. When was the last time in your professional life you were given 75 minutes, no access to outside resources or experts, and asked to demonstrate what you know? We ought to be teaching our students how to manage and access the enormous amounts of information that will be at their fingertips in the decades ahead. This does not mean we should abandon in-class exams, but we need to see exams and the development of test-taking skills in larger professional contexts.

Bearing these principles in mind, consider four types of exams: multiple-choice tests, short-answer and essay exams, problem-solving tests, and open note/book or take-home exams. Other types of exams exist and are described in the reference sources listed at the end of the chapter, but these four are the ones new teachers usually turn to first. Each type of test has advantages (which often imply disadvantages), and some particulars associated with their use. Most also can be used innovatively.

Multiple-Choice Items

With multiple-choice items, an instructor can cover a wide range of content. Contrary to common belief, multiple-choice items can be written so that they test multiple levels of learning. These questions can be answered and scored quickly, which makes them an efficient choice in large classes.

As for particulars, multiple-choice items, especially those that test higher-level learning skills, such as the ability to integrate, evaluate, and synthesize, are very difficult to write. Most instructors end up with items that test memory and recall because they are so much simpler to prepare.

Because good items are difficult to write, it is wise to consider saving them so that they can be reused. Some faculty keep their students' exams on file in their offices and allow students to review their exams during regular office hours. The approach gives students the opportunity to learn from their mistakes and at the same time allows the instructor the possibility of reusing some items.

Many universities and even most colleges have some sort of university testing or computer center where exams can be machine scored. Using the service saves the instructor time, increases the accuracy of the scoring and, most important, allows analysis of the individual items. Using a variety of simple and easy to understand statistical tests, these staff members can provide data that will show how well the questions are working, thereby making the decision of which questions to keep, which to revise, and which to toss an informed choice.

Advice on constructing multiple-choice items abounds and ought to be followed by teachers who are new to the test construction business. The following checklist developed by John Ory, coauthor of the book on testing in this series (Ory & Ryan, 1993), provides a useful set of beginning guidelines.

Multiple-Choice Question Checklist

When possible, the author:

_____ stated the item as a direct question rather than as an incomplete statement.

_____ presented a definite, explicit, and singular question or problem in the stem.

_____ eliminated excessive verbiage or irrelevant information from the stem.

_____ included in the stem any word(s) that might have otherwise been repeated in each alternative.

_____ used negatively stated stems sparingly. When used, underlined and/or capitalized the negative word(s).

_____ made all alternatives plausible and attractive to the less-knowledgeable or skillful student.

_____ made the alternatives grammatically parallel with each other, and consistent with the stem.

_____ made the alternatives mutually exclusive.

_____ when possible, presented alternatives in some logical order (e.g., chronologically; most to least).

_____ made sure there was only one correct or best response per item.

_____ made alternatives approximately equal in length.

_____ avoided irrelevant clues such as grammatical structure, well-known verbal associations, or connections between stem and answer.

_____ used at least four alternatives for each item.

_____ randomly distributed the correct response among the alternative positions throughout the test, having approximately the same proportion of alternatives a, b, c, d, and e as the correct response.

_____ used the alternatives "none of the above" and "all of the above" sparingly. When used, such alternatives were occasionally the correct answer.

As for creative alternatives, consider the group exam example described in Chapter 4 or something less ambitious, such as including one blank question on the exam. Ask students to write the multiple-choice item (or short-answer question or problem, for that matter) they had hoped would be on the exam but that did not appear. This simple strategy gives students the opportunity to demonstrate something they do know or have prepared for the exam.

Short-Answer/Essay Exams

These exams have the advantage of testing complex learning outcomes. They allow an instructor to explore students' thought processes and at the same time require students to use and develop their writing skills. The questions themselves require much less time to prepare than multiple-choice items, and they minimize student guessing.

There are a plethora of difficulties associated with grading short-answer tests and essays. In the first place, any time saved in preparing the questions is more than consumed in grading the answers. Students benefit most from prompt and immediate feedback, which is extraordinarily difficult to provide when faced with a large number of exams. Some professors engage in marathon grading sessions, but the success of this method is much like that of the term paper written in one night. The quality of feedback and indeed the fairness of the grading usually suffers.

Unfortunately, studies in a variety of different fields have established the fact that we are not very reliable graders of essays and short answers. We are influenced by our knowledge of the student and how we expect that individual to perform. We may be distracted by grammar and spelling. In some cases we are even influenced by where the student's paper is in the stack.

The advice for overcoming these potentially serious problems involves approaching the grading task systematically. Some recommend outlining the essentials of an A, B, C, and so on, answer before reading the exams. Others recommend reading all the answers and generally sorting them before actually assigning grades. The references offer more advice, but it can all be summed up with the reminder that we are not always as objective as we should be.

As for creative alternatives, one faculty member I know attaches a copy of the essay final exam to the syllabus he distributes on the first day. With a smile, he tells the students, "See, this way you don't have to spend the whole semester worrying about what's going to be on the final in this course. You already know." Students then answer a randomly selected set of the 50 questions during the final.

Problem-Solving Exams

Tests where students solve problems have the advantage of better approximating reality, since many jobs involve solving problems. These exams also give students the opportunity to apply existing knowledge to new situations. In order to make those applications, they must really understand the content. Problems permit instructors to give credit for partial knowledge. The answer may still be wrong, but the student may have been headed in the right direction. Getting at least some credit can be especially encouraging for beginning students or those not doing particularly well in the course. Problems are relatively easy to make up and are amendable to small revisions that essentially make them new problems, so keeping the questions secure is much less of a problem.

As for particulars, the thorniest ones have to do with developing students' problem-solving abilities. Students often do not accept the fact that these abilities develop in the context of repeated practice. They manage to persuade themselves that they can conquer this kind of course as they have courses in other disciplines—by cramming the day and night before the exam. They do poorly and often do not see their study strategy as the culprit.

Some faculty use graded homework assignments and/or quizzes as a way of encouraging the necessary practice. Others try tackling the problem in a more up-front manner. One physics professor told me that he has students who succeeded in his course write short notes of advice to incoming students. These he distributes with study guides shortly before the first exam. Of course, the notes all say to do the homework, come to class, keep up, work on the material all the time—the same things he would say—but it is received differently when the person delivering the advice recently got an A in the course.

One other particular: Students get very frustrated and disheartened by exam problems that are unlike others they have seen previously. The solution would be to have the homework problems or ones just like them on the exam. An instructor needs to strike a balance and, even more important, needs to give students an opportunity to apply what they have learned to new problems *in class*. There, under considerably less stressful conditions, the appropriate processes can be discussed and the possible approaches can be assessed.

One widely used creative approach to these exams involves allowing students to bring to the exam a 3-by-5-inch card or "crib sheet" on which they have written any information they think they might need on the exam. Generally this is information that is readily accessible in any reference book to which an on-the-job problem solver would have access. Some faculty have students turn the card in with the exam and may use it to show students where they did or did not have the information needed. Preparing the card teaches students some important lessons about prioritizing and integrating information.

A few faculty have given students the option of "making a final or taking a final." Those who make a final are graded on the choice of problems they select for the exam, the relative weight given those problems, and their solutions to them. Students who complete this option frequently report that it took longer to make a final than to prepare to take one.

Open Note/Book or Take-Home Exams

This exam strategy has the advantage of significantly reducing student anxiety. It generally results in better writing than what appears in short answers and in-class essays. It also approximates reality and has the potential to teach some very important information management skills.

In addition to all the grading problems described earlier for short answers and essays, students are often poorly prepared to handle these exams and frequently underestimate the time and skills involved. Faculty who opt to use these exams must almost by necessity be willing to devote class time and other assigned work to developing these skills. For example, students can be given samples of good and poor answers and the opportunity to discuss the differences. A day's lecture can end 10 minutes early with students being given the remaining time to prepare a one-paragraph summary of the day's key points. Groups can discuss and outline the main ideas in a reading assignment.

Feedback That Improves Performance

Finally, with any type of exam, we need to consider the impact of our feedback on subsequent learning, both for the individual student and for the class as a whole. Individual students need balanced feedback. We tend to give them much more criticism than praise. Generally, poor total exam performance needs to be reflected in the comments, but even then, if there is an answer with promise, one that starts in the right direction, or one that makes a minor but articulate point, that needs to be noted.

Students can be overloaded with too much feedback, particularly by motivated and well-meaning new teachers. Especially with poor performances, it is easy to give the students so much feedback that they have no sense of where to begin, and of all students these are the ones most in need of a game plan. It is better to spend time with these students discussing study approaches and processes than to overload them with too much feedback on a poor performance. Subsequently, the teacher should make special note of student improvement even if that progress has not yet resulted in an unusually high mark. All of this advice rests on a single premise: Feedback to students has important consequences related to the effort and energy they expend learning your course content.

In addition to feedback to individual students, feedback can and should be delivered to the class so that their collective performance on exams, and in class for that matter, may improve. This is the time to talk *generally*: which items were missed most often, what mistakes were made most frequently, and what was handled well. This is not the time to respond to a specific question about the details of an individual student's answer.

Sometimes important points about note-taking, study of reading material, and/or completion of homework problems can be made during exam debriefs. I observed once in a class where the instructor noted an item frequently missed and then had the class turn to their notes of November 4 when that topic was discussed. He asked them, "What do you have written down about this?" Some had nothing. Some had a key work but nothing that defined it or noted its significance. One student had most of what was needed for the answer but clearly had no understanding of the context. As the instructor queried further the student fessed up to having not been in class that day. He had gotten the notes from another student. The discussion allowed the instructor to make a number of key points about how having notes does not necessarily mean you are covered.

When discussing exam results in class, teachers need to have thought through how they will deal with contested items. It generally happens like this: A student who missed an item proposes an alternative option and articulates a reasonably defensible argument on its behalf. As you pause to ponder the point, heads all around the room nod, "Yeah, that's what I thought, too." It's hard not to be a bit cynical about some of the nodding heads, but do you give credit there on the spot for that option? If you do, lots of discussion of other items and options will follow. Students can be extremely aggressive when it comes to getting extra points. It is hard not to respond defensively and emotionally once you begin to feel as though you are being taken to the laundry.

You can defer the decision. After making students work for the point, as in asking a number of them to repeat, reiterate, and elaborate the alternative argument and carefully noting what they say, then you can decide in the quiet of the office. Announce your decision and the rationale behind it in class the next day. Any further discussion can occur during office hours. Another strategy involves having students prepare a written and documented case for the option and giving credit selectively, based on the merit of the individual's argument.

If the news about class performance on an exam is bad, a discussion in class needs to explore the reasons why. This relates to the earlier point about teachers needing to worry about their role in student performance. The students and the teacher need to figure out what can be done to prevent what has occurred from being repeated on the next exam. What will they do? What will you do?

Assessing Their Learning: Written Work

Written work includes papers of all sizes and sorts plus more. The Writing-Across-the-Curriculum movement has taught us that any writing exercise, whether it is completed in class or outside, whether it is graded or not, whether it is formal or informal, helps to develop thinking skills. As we sort through the words and phrases we need to explain or explore an idea, our understanding of the concept enlarges and becomes clearer. So, we need to encourage students to write for this reason and also because many of them need the practice.

Student learning can be assessed via a wide range of writing assignments which run the gamut from the formal, generally long term paper to informal paragraphs written in class in response to a discussion or a reading or entries in a learning log that chronicles efforts to master the material. It is important for teachers who are used to thinking about assignments as graded to realize that important feedback about student learning (or the lack of it) can also appear on ungraded written assignments.

To explore assessing learning via written work, consider several general principles.

❶ *Decide on the degree to which writing counts versus the degree to which content counts.* The decision depends on the nature of the individual assignment. If you are having students write a short paper in class whose contents they will share in a small group discussion, the quality of the writing need not count at all. However, if the writing in an essay answer obfuscates the point being made, then the writing should count against the answer. The decision also depends on the level and ability of the students. If they are beginning a college career and don't have adequate writing skills, they need to understand that their writing ability does not measure up, but the writing may need to count less as they struggle to develop those skills. For them, it may be important that the instructor make an extra effort to wade through a rambling, somewhat fragmented paragraph in search of their point. The decision should not depend on your skill as a grammarian. You can still respond to student writing even if you miss dangling participles, split infinitives, or the misuse of the past perfect. Students often do not know these grammatical fine points either, so pointing them out is not necessarily useful feedback. Rather, students need to know if they have clearly communicated an idea, whether their argument was understood. If not, you need to point that out in terms of individual sentences and paragraphs. Writing should count when it enhances or prevents your understanding of student learning. This decision need not be a definitive one, as in writing counts 40% and content 60%. Rather, you need to be aware of the interplay between writing style and content and the extent to which they affect and are influenced by each other.

❷ *Work to demystify the writing process.* Writing assignments raise student anxiety levels. They are not usually confident, empowered writers. For them good writing is a mystery, an art for which they have no natural abilities. It helps them enormously to have the process broken down into steps consisting of concrete tasks. With entry-level students and longer papers, most faculty have found that having a paper due in parts—the topic, list of resources, outline, first draft, revised draft, and final version—makes the assignment seem less daunting and improves the quality of the paper.

❸ *Consider the size of the assignments.* You need to decide on the length and number of writing assignments, partly in terms of the learning needs of your students and partly in terms of your grading load. Beginning students who have little writing experience and who lack skills and confidence cope poorly with the large, end-of-course term paper. Shorter papers provide students with more feedback and more opportunities to develop paper writing skills. The point is not to abolish term papers but to prepare students to write them well.

Feedback That Improves Performance

As with exams, the feedback for written work needs to be aimed at both the individual student and the class as a whole. Again, faculty need to work to provide balanced feedback to individual students, feedback that is specific and concrete in describing what students need to do to improve and further feedback that then notes improvement.

With written work, students can provide one another with valuable feedback. Some faculty assign students to writing groups that meet regularly throughout the course. Students use these groups to test out ideas on others, have outlines reviewed and drafts discussed. To insure that groups spend time on the task assigned, you can have students prepare a journal that summarizes the feedback received from the group and how the student modified papers accordingly.

In providing feedback to individual students, it is important to remember how vested they are in their work. Writing communicates who we are and what we think. It is hard but necessary to separate the self from the writing. We need to help students understand that when we grade a piece of writing harshly, we are providing feedback on a performance, not on a person.

As for feedback to the class, obviously you can offer general comments and suggestions. You can also be explicit about the criteria and demonstrate the grading process. Putting a sample paper on overheads and grading it in front of the students, speaking aloud the thoughts and reactions you have as you read it, shows them that the process is not a mysterious one.

Assessing Their Learning: Projects, Presentations, and Performances

In fields such as art and music, students most often demonstrate their mastery of material via a performance or some tangible display of what they have learned. These can be the most accurate demonstrations of learning because students do not just report on what they know, they show it. That is the principle advantage of these vehicles of assessment.

In addition, projects, presentations, and performances are frequently completed by a group of students who, through the experience, may learn important lessons about shared responsibility, cooperation, and group dynamics.

Like written work, the range of activities within this arena is broad. Students may work individually or collectively on lab projects; presentations may include the preparation of video materials; performances can range from the demonstration of a skill in a physical education class to a class-scripted, one-act play. Even participation in class is a presentation of sorts and is often graded. Because these activities provide such real-life demonstrations of knowledge, faculty in fields where they are not used extensively ought to consider them and seek advice on their use from those who use them regularly.

Consider this general principle: *Work to make the grading criteria explicit.* This is hard because in many cases the assessment depends on an aesthetic evaluation that is the consequence of years of experience. To the seasoned eye or ear it just looks or sounds right. But to students a judgment can seem whimsical or capricious. To deny the role of experience and that aesthetic sense would be dishonest, but we should labor hard to help students understand and emulate it.

Feedback That Improves Performance

For individuals, feedback for these assessment activities is often one-on-one and verbal. In a physical activity course, the instructor works with individuals, often demonstrating a better way of completing a movement. In a graphics design course, student work is frequently shared with and discussed by the entire class.

This last kind of feedback is particularly potent because it is so immediate. The student is also vulnerable—the feedback is public—which makes it particularly important for instructors to have good verbal communication skills. Messages should focus on the work, never on the individual. The painting lacks focus, not the person who painted it. The messages are explicit—not "This piece lacks coherence," but "I don't see how this element here relates to this element here or to the rest of the composition as a whole."

The powerful comments of the teacher can be put into perspective and context if the comments of fellow students are entertained as well. It is unlikely that everyone will respond negatively and even the positive comments of a few can help an aspiring artist view a work more objectively. When providing feedback on a group project, presentation, or performance, it is useful to focus on how the individual pieces fit together into some unified, collective whole that is larger and different from what five separate persons could accomplish alone. Often in my communication courses, group presentations are nothing more than five individuals each speaking on a prescribed part of a topic. Students need to understand that group products need to be more than a sum of individual parts.

Grades

Grades are the tangible, enduring outcome of our assessment of student learning. We make comments and offer feedback, but what endures as a permanent and formal record of student mastery of material is the grade. And our society uses those grades as gatekeepers to a variety of professional schools, graduate education, and that all-important first job. Our students are right to be concerned about their grades. We owe it to them to ensure that those grades are as accurate, valid, and reliable as we can make them. But despite our very best efforts, the grades we give are still imprecise measures of learning and not terribly predictive of any sort of future success.

After having distributed a not so high set of grades, I have been known to circulate my own graduate school transcript. I received an F in a graduate course on Shakespeare. I point out to the students, with only a hint of sarcasm—Isn't it a wonder that I have for better than 20 years been gainfully employed, that I have written books, been happily married, and generally seem to be of at least some worth to society?

The antic makes them smile and I hope puts grades in that larger perspective.

What grading system should you use? One that works for you, is fair to students, and generally does not get in the way of their learning. Most test experts recommend against strict use of a curve. It creates an inflexible template to which every class must conform. Even if you have a class of superstars, you still must grade some below average, and the converse works as well. Besides, grading on the curve creates a competitive classroom environment that pits student against student and makes them less likely to cooperate.

Our comments about grades are brief—not because they are trivial but because we have chosen in this chapter to focus on the assessment of learning and feel an excessive grade orientation makes it easy to lose sight of this larger and infinitely more significant context.

Assessing Your Teaching

Much like students who get personally involved in assessments of their learning, it is easy for teachers to feel the same vulnerabilities when it comes to assessments of their instruction. Rather than thinking about these activities as definitive statements about your inherent worth in the college classroom, you need to see them as attempts to gain feedback and input describing the impact of your instructional policies, practices, and activities on student learning. This is the arena in which we operationalize our premise that how well students learn is tied to, but not exclusively, a function of how well they are taught.

What we are proposing should not be confused with the formal, end-of-course evaluations most institutions conduct to help them make good personnel decisions. That summative information, generally collected via bureaucratically efficient, machine-scorable short forms and distributed to instructors well after a class has concluded has been shown to be marginally ineffective in improving instruction. Institutions have a right to collect it and use in personnel decision making, but individual instructors need data that are more descriptive and less judgmental if they are to assess the impact of their instruction on student learning.

To effectively assess the impact of your teaching on student learning, you need input from three sources; yourself, your students, and your colleagues. Your input is central. When it comes to implementing alterations in the class, you and you alone are the person with the power to do that. Much like you cannot learn material for your students, no one else can improve your instruction.

Feedback From You

How do you think your teaching is affecting student learning? It is a hard question, not easily addressed by a person with a vested interested in the answer. But you are in the best position to know. You are there every day, seeing students, responding to their questions, and assessing their work.

To explore how your teaching is affecting their learning, you need an intense commitment to honesty and as cool, detached, and rational an assessment of your teaching as you can muster. This is not easy for new teachers, who lack experience and the confidence that comes with it. However, if you can avoid several common pitfalls, you can gain the necessary perspective on your teaching.

First, *teachers tend to overgeneralize.* One day in class or one segment of a period goes poorly and the teacher jumps to the comprehensive conclusion, "I can't teach." In fact, you did not teach well one, two, or even ten days in a 15-week course. That still leaves a lot of other days. Moreover, teaching always has variable affects. You try something in class and two or three vocal students object. Chances are, for two or three other students it may have worked well. As we noted in Chapter 6, students learn in different ways. You cannot expect all instructional strategies to work equally well with all students.

Second, *teachers tend to think judgmentally* about their teaching. This tendency overlaps with the first one, but the problem here is not just the comprehensiveness of the conclusion but that *and* the highly judgmental nature of it. The activity worked well; didn't work at all. I did fine; I did poorly. They like me; they don't like me. The problem with the judgments is that they put our self-worth on the line. You need to think more descriptively about your teaching. Recall in Chapter 1 where we proposed how the abstract components of effective instruction are translated into things we do in class. You need to focus on these activities of instruction—try to make the important distinction between the teaching and the person doing the teaching.

Third, *teachers tend to overreact to negative comments.* You do need to take student objections seriously, but you also need to put them in perspective. Several years ago a faculty member called me and sounded in the midst of a major midlife crisis. He had just received a terrible set of evaluations and was devastated. I persuaded him to send me the evaluations and after reading them I wondered if they were his. Of the 38 evaluations, 5 heaped lavish praise on the course, 16 were generally favorable, 10 were a pretty even blend of positive and negative comments and 7 were more negative than positive with only 3 of those outright critical. A set of evaluations like that does not warrant even a modest midlife crisis.

Finally, *too many teachers worry too much about whether or not their students like them.* Some faculty make loud, public pronouncements about how they do not care what students think of them, but most of us do and to some degree should. The research is pretty clear that the kind of rapport we establish with students does influence their learning. If they respond positively to us, their motivation increases, which means they work harder and generally learn more. The problem results when we approximate teaching to some sort of popularity contest, and being liked becomes an anxiety that influences our ability to make sound educational choices. The question a teacher should ask when assessing instruction is not "Do my students like me?" but "How are my instructional policies, practices, strategies, and techniques affecting their learning?" Student learning is the bottom line. Teachers can self-assess. It takes a commitment to honesty and work to avoid these mistakes, but with those two prerequisites fulfilled, the assessment of instructional activities inevitably generates questions that feedback from students and colleagues can help to answer.

Feedback From Students

Feedback from students can be acquired via methods generally categorized as formal or informal. Formal methods principally employ some sort of paper and pencil instrument that students complete. However, these instruments can be creative, innovative, even tailor-made. Plenty of instruments already exist, so they need not be made from scratch but can be assembled by borrowing some questions from other instruments, revising others, and writing some of your own. Tailor-made instruments ask questions relevant to your teaching, students, and instructional situation.

The most useful information comes from questions that are concrete and specific. It is fine to get some input on student perceptions of your attitude toward teaching the course, if that interests you, but it's better to discover if your lectures facilitate note taking. You can improve your lecture structure and students' note-taking skills much easier than you can fix some unnamed attitude.

Instruments use either open or closed questions. In response to the later students generally mark on a scale indicating the degree to which they do or do not agree with the item. With open questions, a wide range of answers are possible. Responses to questions like, "How effective were the exams in measuring what you feel you were learning in the course?" should be mined for good ideas and insights, not generalizations. If you want an "average" or "general sense" of the classes responses, use a closed question form that will allow you to calculate means and standard deviations. In addition to formal instruments that many experts recommend administering intermittently throughout the course, you should consider a whole range of more informal feedback mechanisms. Some faculty regularly use a reaction sheet or minute-paper approach on which they solicit an anonymous student response to a particular instructional event or shorter period of instruction. "Give me some feedback on the film we saw Tuesday. Should I continue to use it? Why? Why not?" Or, "Tell me about your experiences with the readings this week. Any passages particularly difficult, relevant, or interesting? How much time did you spend on the readings this week? Are you using the study questions?" Questions are geared not to find out whether the student "likes" a strategy but to discover how it affected learning. Other faculty solicit similar student commentary via a suggestion/question box or via e-mail.

This is input to be quickly read and assessed, not agonized over. These are methods that allow one to keep a finger on the pulse of a class—which is particularly difficult in large classes. They open lines of communication and make the students and their teacher more mindful of how instructional processes impact on learning.

What can you do to ensure that you get good quality input from students? The answer is simpler than you might suspect and gives students more credit than many faculty normally do. You get good input by regularly and routinely asking for it. This is not a once-in-a-course event but an ongoing practice that is part of the class. Next you respond to what students provide, and finally you tell them what you intend to do in response to their comments.

That last statement sometimes makes faculty go pale. They imagine a majority of the class recommending courses without exams and wonder if classes are like democracies where the majority rules. They are not. You can, and in some cases legitimately should, veto what students propose. When you do, students need to understand why. What is the educational rationale behind your decision? You can also explore with them how you might better prepare them to cope with these instructional events.

So, you insure quality input from students by asking for it, responding to it, and finally by using it. If students see you making changes that respond to their needs, they know that you have a vested interest in providing meaningful input and will contribute mightily. Pretty soon it is no longer "your" class or even "their" class, but it has become "our" class where responsibility for teaching and learning belong to everyone.

Feedback From Colleagues

As important as input from students is, it comes from one perspective, that of the learner. Despite its centrality, learners in courses for grades have certain biases. You can balance the student viewpoint with your own perspective as teacher, but you can balance it even further if you seek input from your colleagues as well.

An unfortunate norm exists in some quarters of higher education. According to that norm, talk about teaching should be superficial, perfunctory, and never personal. In this academic culture appropriate instructional topics include the decline of students and the lack of reward for teaching. In these environments, teaching occurs in isolation behind doors that are closed as tightly as bathroom and bedroom doors. And, instructional quality suffers as a consequence.

We need to engage colleagues in efforts to understand and improve instruction. To begin, quite simply, we need to engage our colleagues in meaningful, intellectually robust conversations about teaching and learning. These conversations may occur about a particular event that has taken place in class. They may be about larger philosophical issues like those lurking in notions of value-added education or the concept of a core curriculum. The conversations may be in response to an instructional article or book you have both agreed to read. Whatever the vehicle, we use conversations with colleagues to test the assumptions and premises on which our educational practice rests.

We should engage our colleagues in review and assessment of instructional materials, be that our syllabi, reading lists, handouts, overheads, exams, graded papers, or any other item students use in their efforts to learn course content. Colleagues from our discipline can respond to the propriety, relevance, and currency of their content. Colleagues in other disciplines provide the perspective of experienced learners and the questions of someone unfamiliar with the content. Both responses are useful.

What we ask of our colleagues is not a definitive judgment but a descriptive reaction. "After having looked at this syllabus, what would you conclude about the course and its instructor?" "What questions would you want to raise?" Frequently, if you ask colleagues to respond to your materials they will share theirs. With the many common instructional tasks that transcend disciplines, we have much to learn from the experiences of one another.

Colleagues can be particularly helpful in our efforts to respond fairly and objectively to a set of student evaluation data. They may interpret a student comment completely differently than we do. If we tend to fixate on the negative comments, they can remind us of the positive ones. Obviously, a certain vulnerability occurs when you share this feedback. It is important that you select a colleague you can trust and not one who can or will subsequently use what is learned against you.

Finally, we should engage our colleagues in instructional observations. This is the most frightening and frequently avoided contact—probably made that way by the kind of commando raid observations that often occur as part of the personnel decision-making process. This is a most unfortunate use of colleagues, decried by many researchers who have shown that these single-class observations completed by faculty who do not regularly observe instructions are not very reliable. We can and should make better use of our colleagues. Consider the following approaches and alternatives.

New faculty particularly benefit from the chance to observe experienced and effective instructors. You ask to observe them teach not in order to make any sort of judgment but to see firsthand how they confront the same instructional issues that you face. Or, you ask them to observe your class. You can help them resist their predilection to judge by offering them a checklist to complete or by identifying specific areas in which you would like their feedback. Repeating our now familiar refrain, you are not interested in how well they "liked" anything, but rather you solicit their opinions as to how it affected learning—theirs and the students they observed.

If instructional observation sounds like a wonderful idea but in your heart of hearts you know you won't do it, consider videotaping as an alternative. Even if it is a taped sample of someone else teaching, you and a colleague can learn much about instructional approaches by watching and discussing it together. Frequently that process motivates you to have your own class taped. Again, a colleague can be an invaluable source of insight and objectivity as you review the tape. If you both agree to be taped and to spend time with each other's tapes, the mutual vulnerability will protect you both.

The notion of colleagues as we understand it in higher education is unique among the professions. It implies a high order, mutually beneficial professional (and sometimes personal) friendship. Our scholarly work is enriched by intellectual muscling in which colleagues engage. Our teaching could benefit in exactly the same way. So, take a deep breath, suck in your gut, head down the hall, and ask that person who looks a whole lot like a potential colleague if he or she would mind chatting about some things that are happening in your class.

Input from students and colleagues can confirm, elaborate, explain, and correct our self-assessments of instruction. They help us develop the honesty and objectivity necessary for accurate self-assessment. Most important, they help us constructively explore and better understand the crucial link between our teaching and their learning.

Background Reading

Jacobs, L. C., & Chase, C. I. (1992). *Developing and using tests effectively: A guide for faculty.* San Francisco: Jossey-Bass.

Weimer, M., Kerns, M. M., & Parrott, J. L. (1988). *How am I teaching?* Madison, WI: Magna.

8 | Conclusion

From some perspectives disarmingly simple, the various techniques, strategies, and approaches of teaching belie much greater depth and complexity. Success in the classroom does begin with techniques. To get students involved in a discussion, for example, you need as many techniques as you can find. They should be committed to memory and planned into the lesson. But the complexity emerges the moment those strategies are implemented. You try one and it does not work. Which of the 14 others at your disposal should you turn to next? You select one, more intuitively than reflectively—you don't have time to think through to a reasoned choice. It doesn't work. Now living with the consequences of two unsuccessful attempts, you must select a third.

About this teaching-in-action, Elliot Eisner (1983) writes,

> I suggest that it is in this space—the interstices between framework and action—that the art and craft of teaching is most crucial. We face a class, we raise a question, we get little or no response. Theoretical frameworks and the findings of research studies provide only limited help. What we do is to look for cues.

In Eisner's observation is another message. Much of what makes teaching successful we have yet to discover. Yes, we know the components. In this book we have discussed them in terms of techniques and in terms of issues that are inherently a part of how they function. The tools are here—yours for the taking. You cannot teach well without them, but you may not teach successfully even with them. Said simply: We have much left to learn.

A book on teaching marks a point of departure. You begin by responding to its contents. You now have strategies to try out. The introduction to additional resources opens the door to further interaction with them. The unanswered questions serve to stimulate additional thought and dialogue.

Said with a bit more candor, you do not know all that is necessary if your teaching is to regularly result in student learning. But you already know more than many faculty. You have read a book on teaching and a sizeable number of those teaching today cannot make that claim. However, let this be the first of a series of continuing, systematic efforts to develop both classroom skills and an appreciation of the complexities involved in the process.

The continuing devaluation of teaching is cause for concern. How can something so central to the mission of our institution, so intrinsically a part of the advancement of knowledge be given such short shrift? The answer is complicated, but I am firmly convinced that the lack of reward and recognition in part results from the simplistic, nonreflective, and uninformed ways many in our profession think about teaching. Approaching the teaching-learning enterprise in more intellectually robust ways puts you on the side of those of us committed to being part of the solution. It also sets you up to appreciate and better understand the joy, wonder, and intrigue that are a part of teaching at its best.

References

Amstutz, J. (1988). In defense of telling stories. *The Teaching Professor, 2*(4), 5.

Barnett, D. C., & Dalton, J. C. (1981). Why college students cheat. *Journal of College Student Personnel, 22,* 545-551.

Bonwell, C. C., & Eison, J. A. (1991). *Active learning: Creating excitement in the classroom.* ASHE-ERIC Higher Education Report No. 1. Washington, DC: The George Washington University, School of Education and Human Development.

Boyer, E. L. (1990). *Scholarship reconsidered: Priorities of the professoriate.* Princeton, NJ: The Princeton University Press.

Brown, G. A. (1978). *On lecturing and explaining.* London: Methuen.

Carrier, C. A. (1983). Notetaking research: Implications for practice. *Journal of Instructional Development, 6*(3), 19-26.

Cross, K. P., & Angelo, T. A. (1988). *Classroom assessment techniques: A handbook for faculty.* Ann Arbor: National Center for Research to Improve Postsecondary Teaching and Learning.

Eisner, E. W. (1983). The art and craft of teaching. *Educational Leadership, 40*(4), 5-13.

Erickson, B. L., & Strommer, D. W. (1991). *Teaching college freshmen.* San Francisco: Jossey-Bass.

Feldman, K. A. (1975). The superior college teacher from the students' view. *Research in Higher Education, 5*(3), 243-288.

Feldman, K. A. (1988). Effective college teaching from the students' and faculty's view: Matched or mismatched priorities. *Research in Higher Education, 28*(4), 291-344.

Gaff, J. G. (1978). Overcoming faculty resistance. In J. G. Gaff (Ed.), *New directions for higher education: Institutional renewal through the improvement of teaching.* San Francisco: Jossey-Bass.

Garcia, R. (1991). Twelve ways of looking at a blackboard. *The Teaching Professor, 5*(8), 5-6.

Keyworth, D. (1989). The group exam. *The Teaching Professor, 3*(8), 5.

Knapper, C. K. (1988). What should future teaching be like? *The Teaching Professor, 2*(2), 1.

Knapper, C. K., & Cropley, A. J. (1985). *Lifelong learning in higher education.* London: Croom Helm.

Kolb, D. A. (1981). Learning styles and disciplinary differences. In A. Chickering (Ed.), *The modern American college* (pp. 232-255). San Francisco: Jossey-Bass.

Lagowski, J. J. (1985). Faith. *Journal of Chemical Education, 62*(10), 821.

Muller, T. E. (1989). Assigning students to groups for class projects: An exploratory test of two methods. *Decision Sciences Journal, 20*(3), 623-634.

Murray, H. (1983). Low-inference classroom teaching behaviors and student ratings of college teaching effectiveness. *Journal of Educational Psychology, 75*(1), 138-149.

Murray, H. (1985). Classroom teaching behaviors related to college teaching effectiveness. In J. Donald & A. Sullivan (Eds.), *New directions for teaching and learning: Using research to improve teaching* (pp. 57-69). San Francisco: Jossey-Bass.

Murray, H. (1987). Acquiring student feedback that improves instruction. In M. Weimer (Ed.), *New directions for teaching and learning: Teaching large classes well* (pp. 85-96). San Francisco: Jossey-Bass.

Ory, J., & Ryan, K. (1993). *Testing and grading: Tips for classroom practice.* Newbury Park, CA: Sage.

Perry, R. (1991). Perceived control in college students: Implications for instruction in higher education. In J. C. Smart (Ed.), *Higher education: Handbook of theory and research* (pp. 1-56). New York: Agathon.

Perry, R., & Penner, K. (1990). Enhancing academic achievement in college students through attributional retraining and instruction. *Journal of Educational Psychology, 82*(2), 262-271.

Rowe, M. B. (1983). Getting chemistry off the killer course list. *Journal of Chemical Education, 60*(11), 954-956.

Schlesinger, A. B. (1986-1987). How do I teach? Let me count the ways. *Creighton University Window,* 15-19.

Schomberg, S. F. (1988). *Strategies for active teaching and learning in university classrooms.* Minneapolis: University of Minnesota.

Sherman, T. M., et al. (1986). The quest for excellence in university teaching. *Journal of Higher Education, 48*(1), 66-84.

Smith, B. L., & MacGregor, J. T. (1992). What is collaborative learning? In A. S. Goodsell, M. R. Maher, & V. Tinto (Eds.), *Collaborative learning: A sourcebook for higher education* (pp. 9-22). University Park, PA: National Center on Postsecondary Teaching, Learning, and Assessment.

Strauss, M., & Fulwiler, T. (1987). Interactive writing and learning in chemistry. *Journal of College Science Teaching, 16*(4), 256-262.

Svinicki, M. D., & Dixon, N. M. (1987). The Kolb model modified for classroom activities. *College Teaching, 35*(4), 141-146.

Welch, L. N. (1991). College students need nurturing too. *The Teaching Professor, 5*(10), 7.

Yelon, S., & Massa, M. (1987, October). Heuristics for creating examples. *Performance and Instruction,* 13-17.

About the Author

Maryellen Weimer is the Associate Director of the National Center on Postsecondary Teaching, Learning, and Assessment, a 5-year, $5.9-million, U.S. Department of Education research and development center. The center, a consortium of six universities, is organizationally and fiscally located within the Center for the Study of Higher Education at Pennsylvania State University where Dr. Weimer is a Senior Research Associate.

Dr. Weimer received her Ph.D. in speech communications from Penn State in 1981. For the next 10 years she directed Penn State's Instructional Development Program.

Her numerous publications include articles in referred journals, book chapters, book reviews, and conference presentations. She serves on the editorial boards of three journals. She has consulted with more than 75 colleges and universities on instructional issues. During the 1991-1992 academic year she keynoted four national conferences.

Dr. Weimer's most recent publications include *Improving College Teaching* (1990). Since 1987 she has edited *The Teaching Professor,* a monthly newsletter on college teaching with 20,000 subscribers.

SURVIVAL SKILLS
FOR SCHOLARS

Place
Stamp
here

SAGE PUBLICATIONS, INC.
P.O. BOX 5084
THOUSAND OAKS, CALIFORNIA 91359-9924